Phaidon Press Limited
140 Kensington Church Street
London W8 4BN

First published in Great Britain 1992

ISBN 0 7148 2816 5

A CIP catalogue record for this book is available from the British Library

Front cover materials courtesy of London Graphic Centre.

Printed in Spain

Learn to draw with

Pencils

Materials, skills and
step-by-step projects

Pencils

Learning to use pencils

This book has been designed to help you learn how to draw with pencils. It tells you about the materials you need and explains the various skills used to create different effects with pencils. Start by reading about the basic skills, then follow the step-by-step projects later in the book to practise and gradually improve what you've learned. Any terms you're not sure of are explained in the glossary at the back of the book.

This book is divided into three parts: the first part tells you about the materials you need; the second part explains the skills for using pencils; the third part contains step-by-step projects to follow.

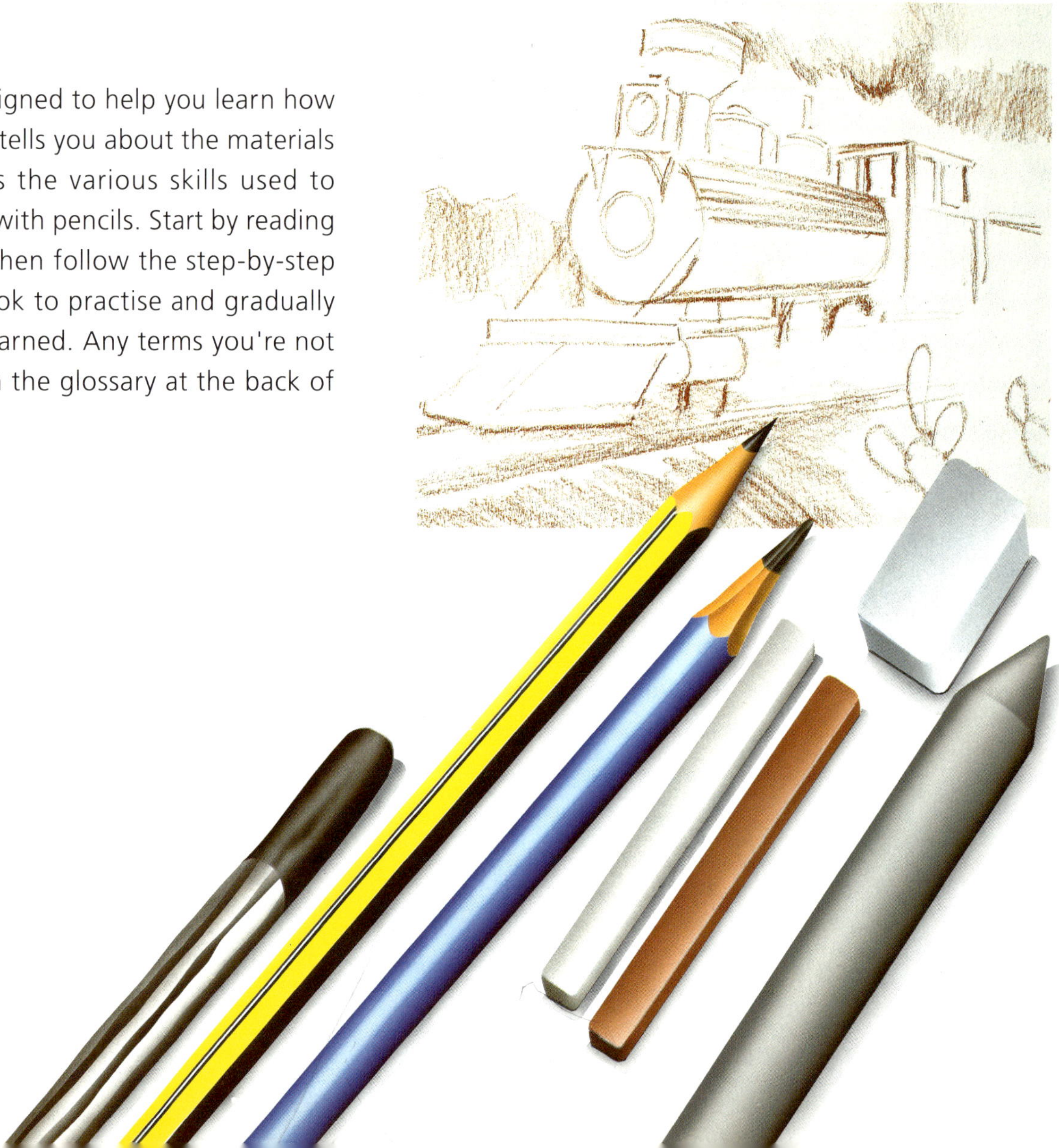

Different types of lead pencils, charcoal pencils, conté crayons and pastels which can be used for drawing.

Basic rules

The basic rules of drawing

There are a few basic rules it is useful to know when learning how to draw. On the following pages you will find detailed explanations of these, and projects to help you practise them. Here's a brief list of the skills explained in this section of the book.

Blocking in. When you begin a drawing, you start by blocking in. This means drawing geometric shapes, such as squares, rectangles, cubes and spheres, to represent the different objects you are drawing.

Dimensions and proportions. Pictures are usually drawn on paper which is smaller than the subject you are drawing. You need to be able to look at the dimensions of what you are drawing - width, height, etc - and then draw a smaller version on paper.

Perspective. The objects around you are not flat - they have three dimensions. The rules of perspective help you to draw an object on flat (or two-dimensional) paper so that it looks three-dimensional.

To draw successfully, you need to learn the basic rules of drawing.

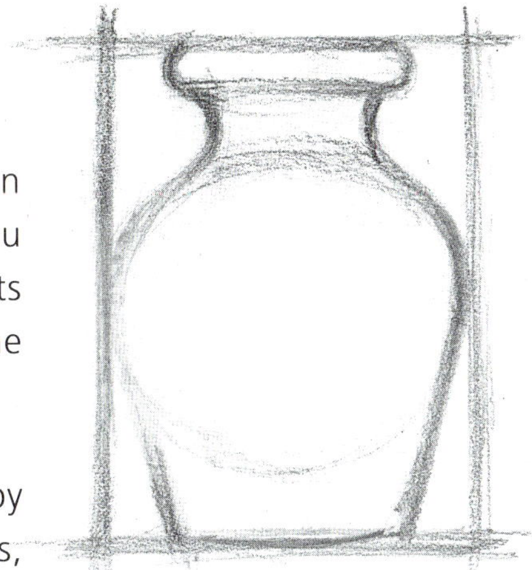

Blocking in the basic shapes

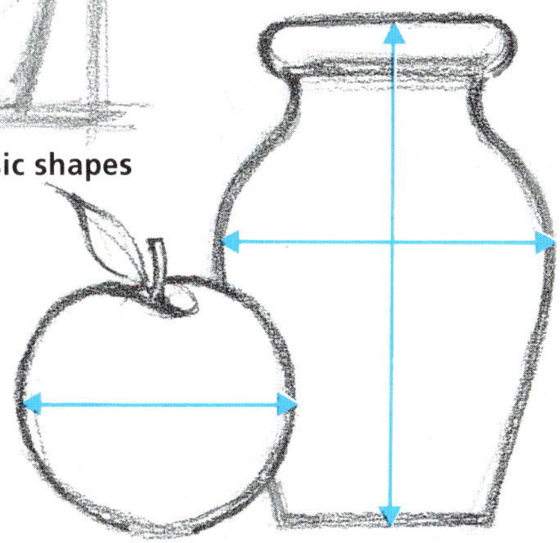

Calculating the dimensions and proportions

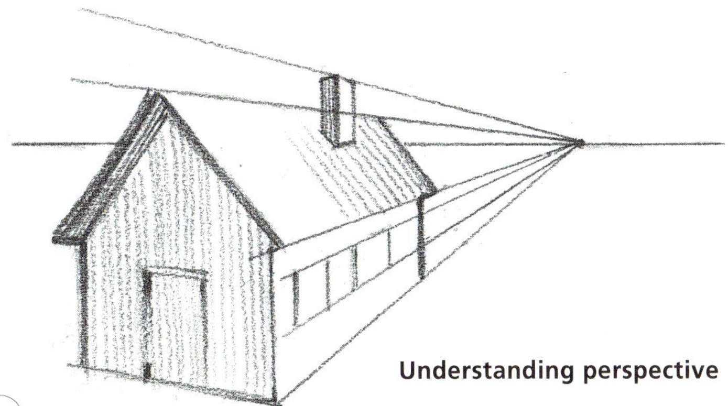

Understanding perspective

Pencils

Lead pencils

These are ordinary pencils, made up of sticks of lead in a wooden casing. Pencil leads are made from graphite and clay. The hardness of the lead depends on how much of each of these materials has been used to make it.

Hard and very hard leads are not often used for drawing. Generally, a mid-range pencil is the best for sketching, and soft ones are used for filling in large areas.

It is a good idea to make a collection of several types of pencil, so that you can draw anything from deep blacks to soft greys.

Your collection should include:

- a 2B or HB for drawing lines
- a 1B or 2B for medium tones
- a 4B or 6B for deep blacks

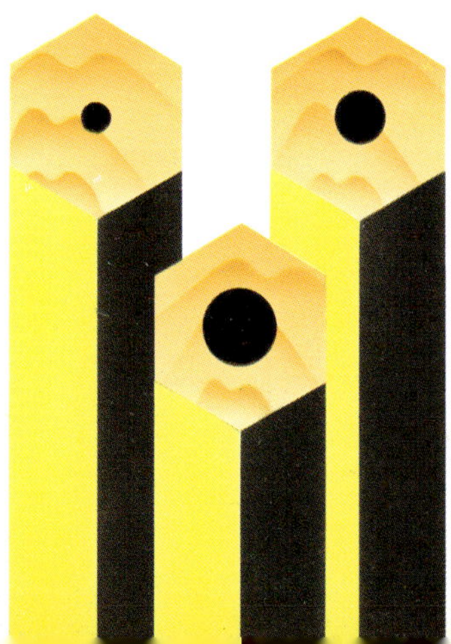

Letters and numbers tell you how hard a lead pencil is.

H *is used for hard pencils and* **B** *for soft ones.* **HB** *and* **F** *are medium range pencils. Sometimes you can tell how hard a pencil is by looking at the thickness of the lead; the thicker it is the softer it will be.*

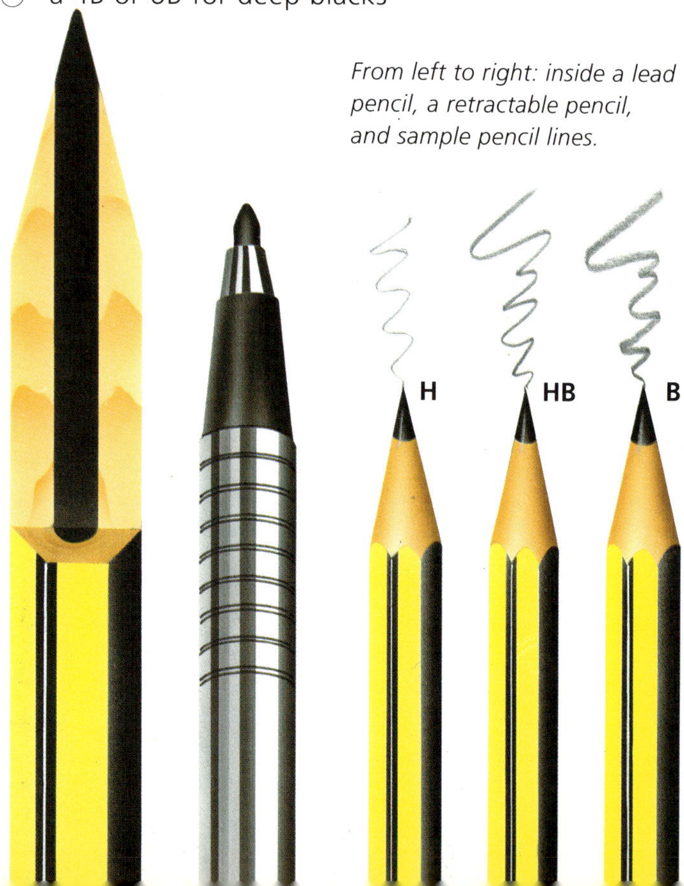

From left to right: inside a lead pencil, a retractable pencil, and sample pencil lines.

How to choose them

Charcoal sticks

Charcoal is made by burning wood. It comes in small sticks about 5-15 mm in diameter. You can draw with a charcoal stick on its own, or in a retractable pencil.

It is easier to use a charcoal pencil than a stick of charcoal. The illustration shows a conté crayon and various coloured pastels.

Charcoal pencils

Like lead pencils, these have a wooden outer casing, with a stick of charcoal inside. You can draw darker lines with a charcoal pencil than with a stick of charcoal.

Pastels

You can buy sticks of white or coloured pastels. They also come in pencil form, with the pastel inside a wooden casing.

Conté crayon

This is a red crayon which contains ferric oxide, a red substance obtained from iron. It can also be called a sanguine crayon.

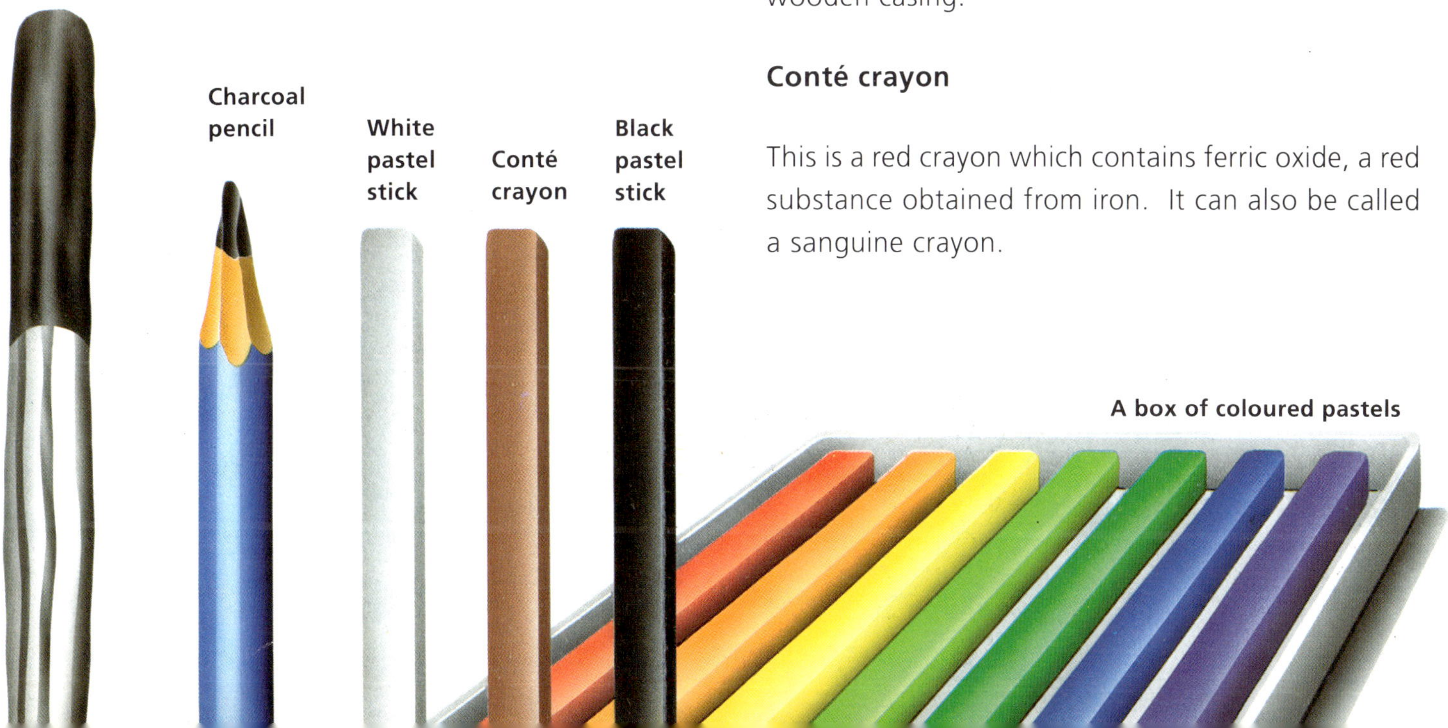

What to draw on

Choosing drawing paper

You can draw on almost any paper, but you will get the best results on paper specially made for drawing. Drawing paper is sold in pads of various shapes and sizes, as well as loose sheets.

What size pad?

To start with buy a fairly small pad. Use it for the projects in this book. You will need to practise the various skills explained in the following pages. Later on, when you are ready to create original drawings of your own, you will need more than one pad so that you can keep a small one for your notes and sketches, and a larger one for your finished pictures.

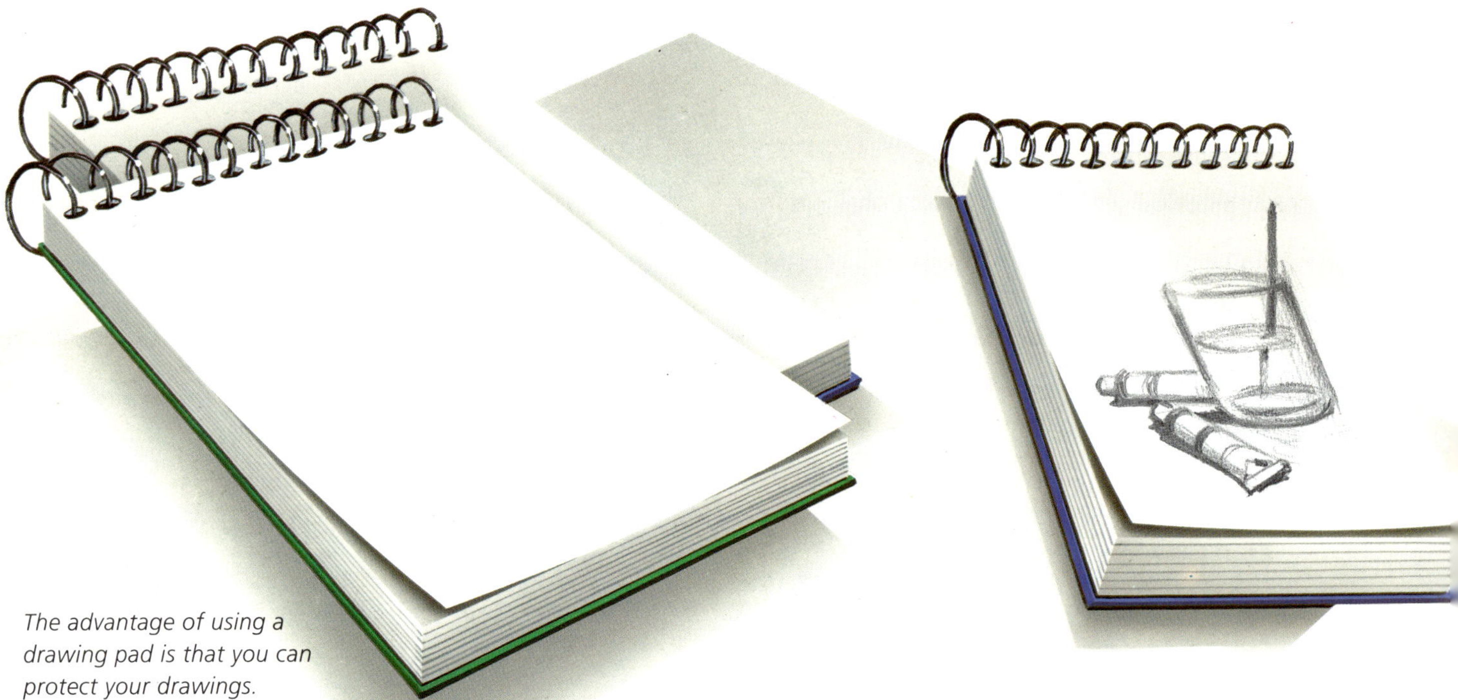

The advantage of using a drawing pad is that you can protect your drawings.

How to choose paper

What sort of paper?

*Three different types of paper: thick grain (**A**), medium grain (**B**), and glossy (**C**), drawn on with soft lead pencil (**1**), medium pencil (**2**), hard pencil (**3**),conté crayon (**4**) charcoal (**5**) and charcoal pencil (**6**).*

Drawing paper comes in many different textures, which give you different types of surface to draw on. Some papers have glossy surfaces, with no grain; others have grainy surfaces which can be fine, medium or thick grain.

- Very glossy paper (the smoothest kind) is not really suitable for pencil drawings. The lead tends to slide on the paper and it is not very easy to rub out lines. Fine grain paper is the best for drawing with pencil.

- When you draw with charcoal, a charcoal pencil or pastels you should use medium or thick grain paper.

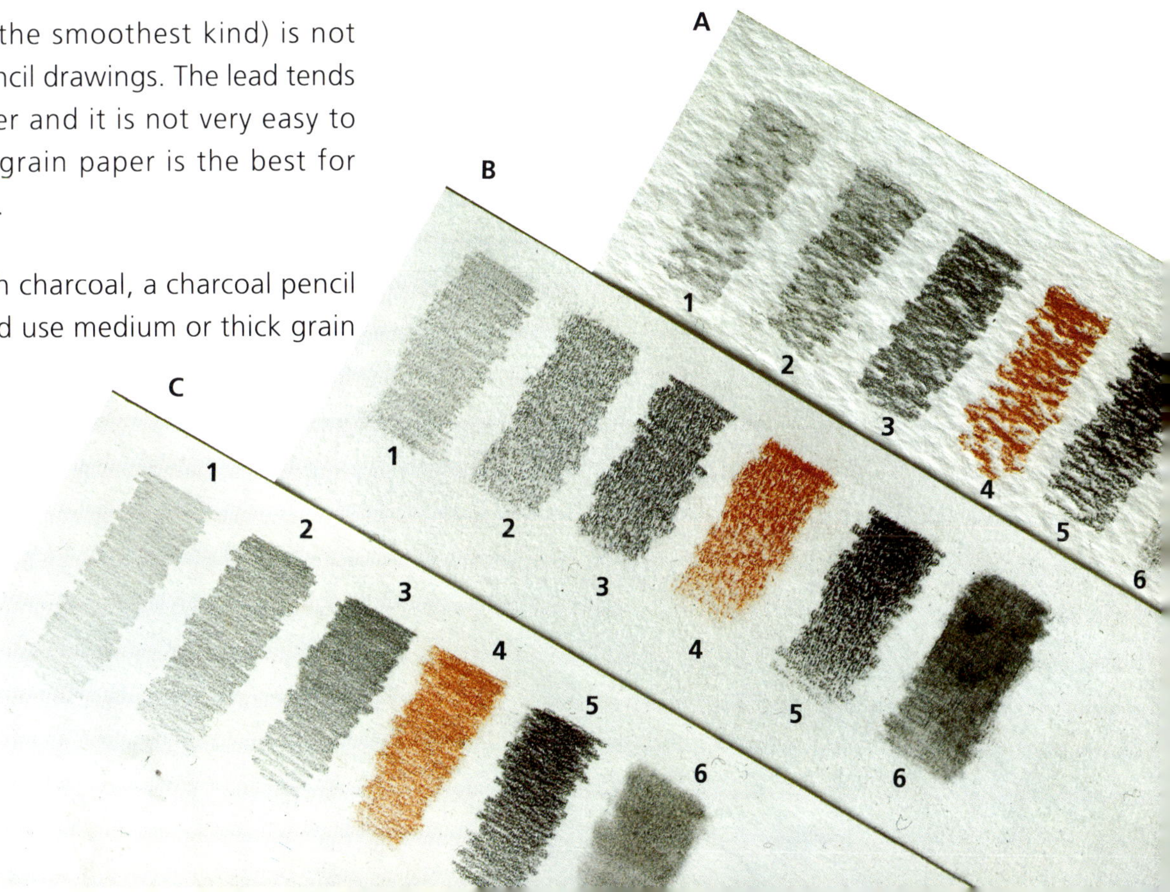

Left: different-sized drawing pads. Use a small pad for your notes and sketches.

Making work easy

A wooden drawing board

You will need a flat surface to lean on when drawing, such as a table. A wooden drawing board, which you can tilt, is an even better surface.

A plywood board about 50 x 70 cm is ideal. Sit with the board on your legs and resting against the edge of the table.

Holding the paper down

If you draw on sheets of paper, pin them in place on the board with four drawing pins in the corners.

A folder about 50 x 65 cm is very useful for storing your pictures, as well as unused sheets of drawing paper.

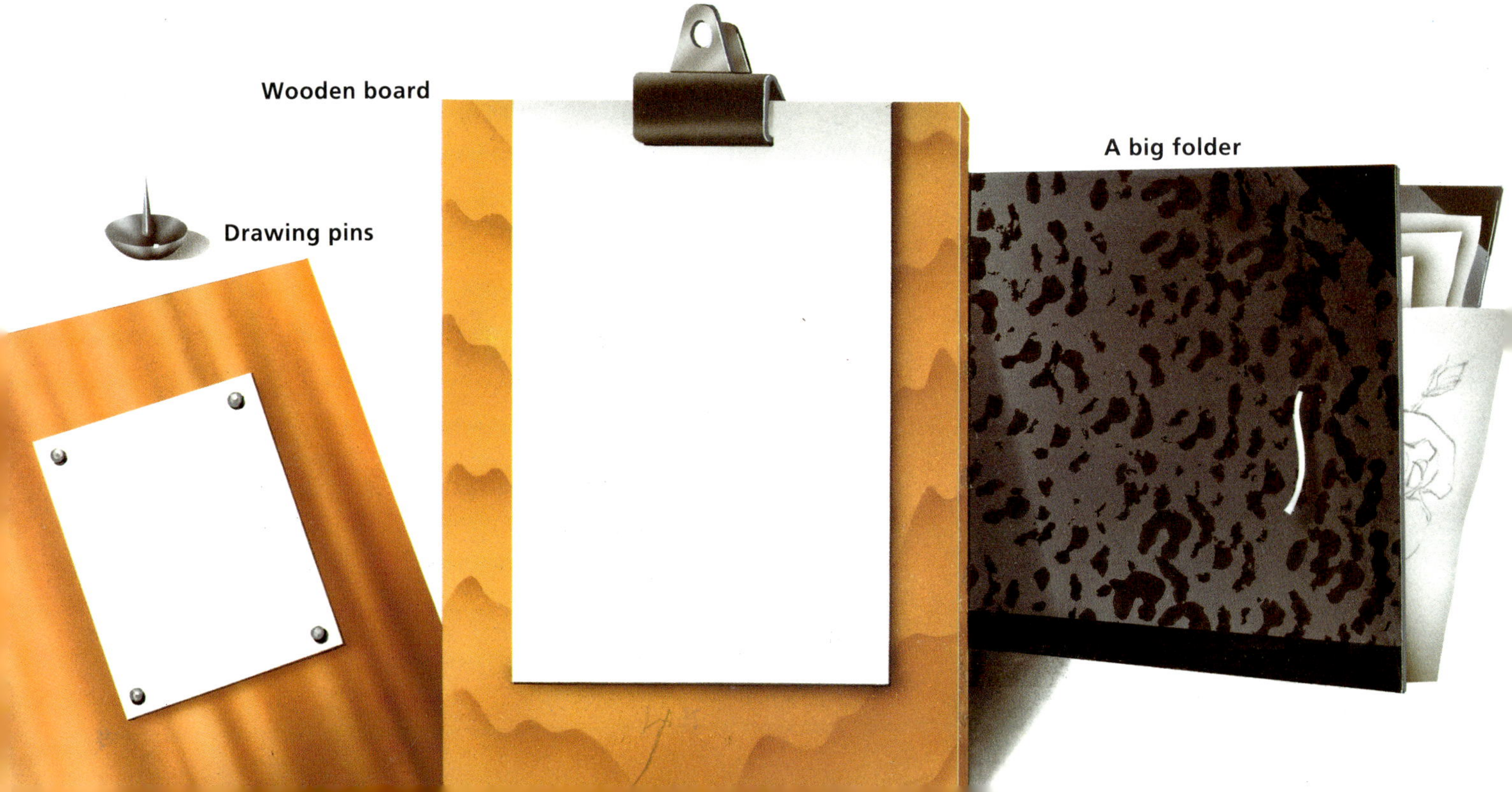

Other tools & materials

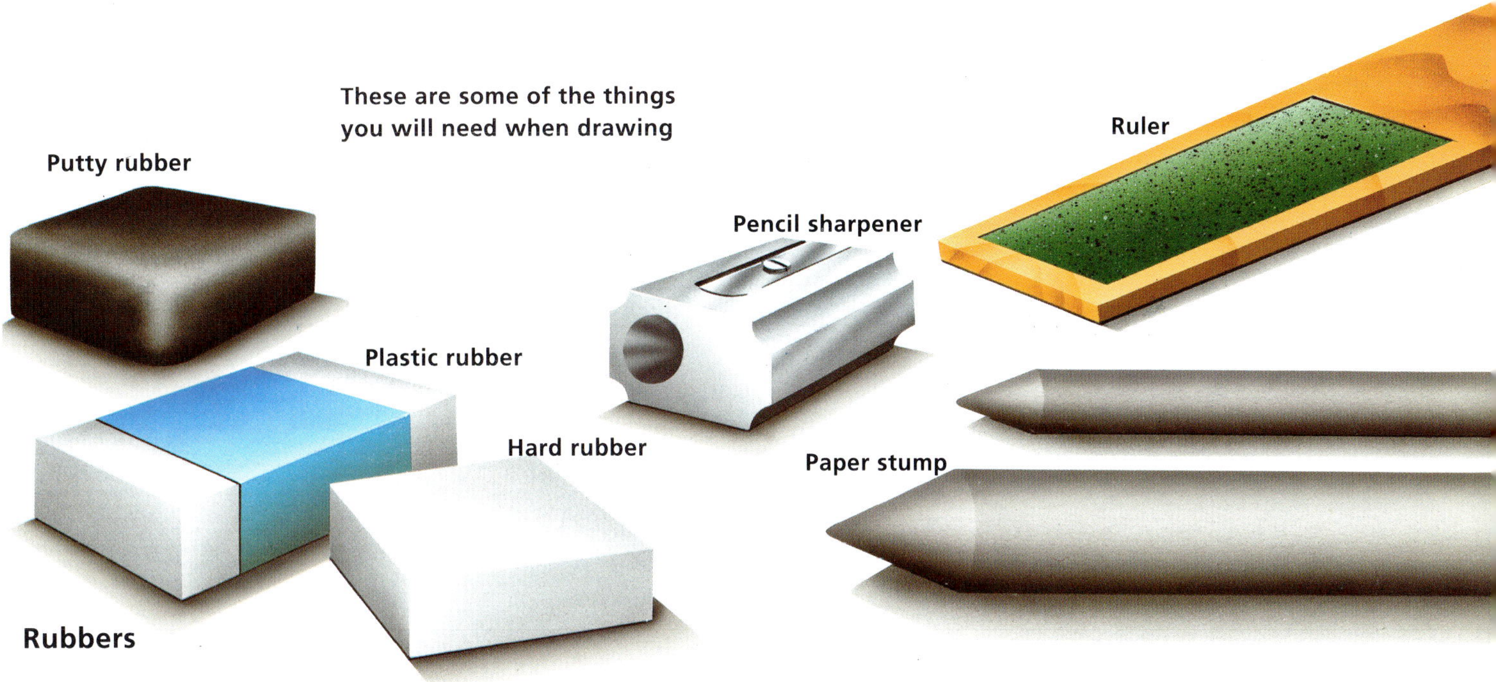

Rubbers

Rubbers are essential when drawing. Apart from rubbing out lines, they can also be used to draw with, as you will see later on in the book.

There are various types of rubbers:

- Plastic rubbers, which are very useful for rubbing out lead pencil
- Hard, compact rubbers
- Putty rubbers - a special type of rubber made from material similar to Plasticine

A pencil sharpener

Make sure that you have a good pencil sharpener. You can use it to sharpen charcoal as well as pencils.

A paper stump

A paper stump is a pointed roll of paper used to spread and even out pencil or chalk lines. You can buy stumps of different thicknesses.

Drawing skills

Holding a pencil

Hold your pencil a little higher than when writing. Don't hold it too tightly; you should draw with a 'loose' hand rather than a stiff one. This is the best grip to use when drawing the main lines of a picture, and putting in the details.

When you are shading large areas put the pencil inside the palm of your hand.

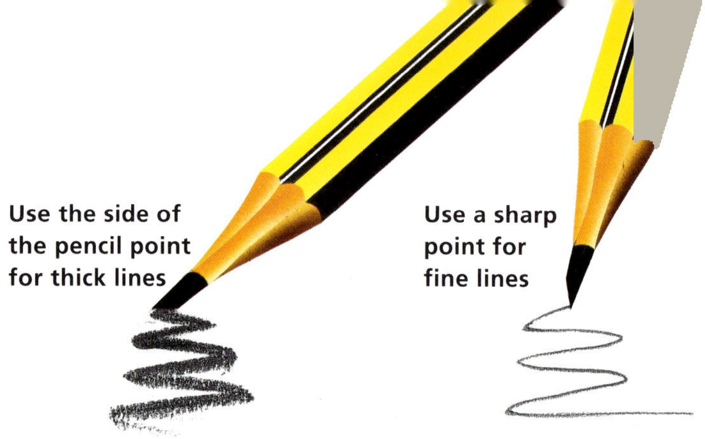

Thick and thin lines

The position of the pencil on the paper determines whether you draw a thick or a thin line. Above you can see thick and thin lines made by holding the pencil at different angles.

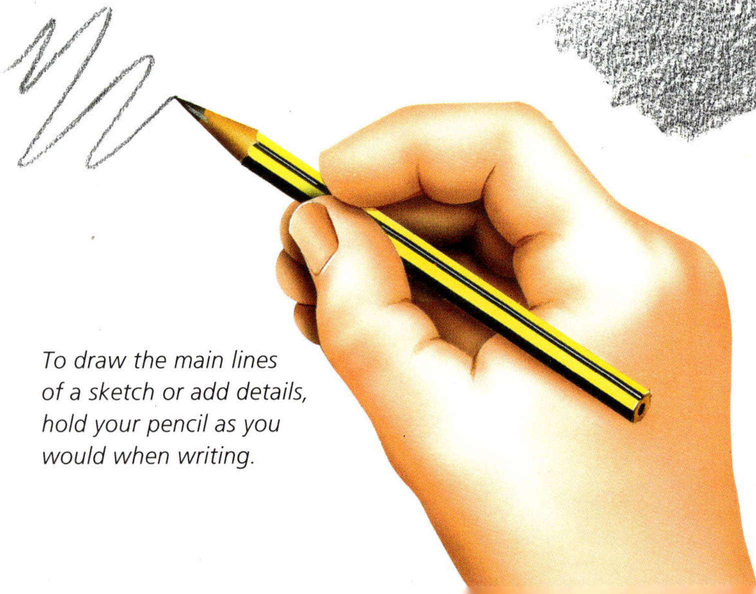

To draw the main lines of a sketch or add details, hold your pencil as you would when writing.

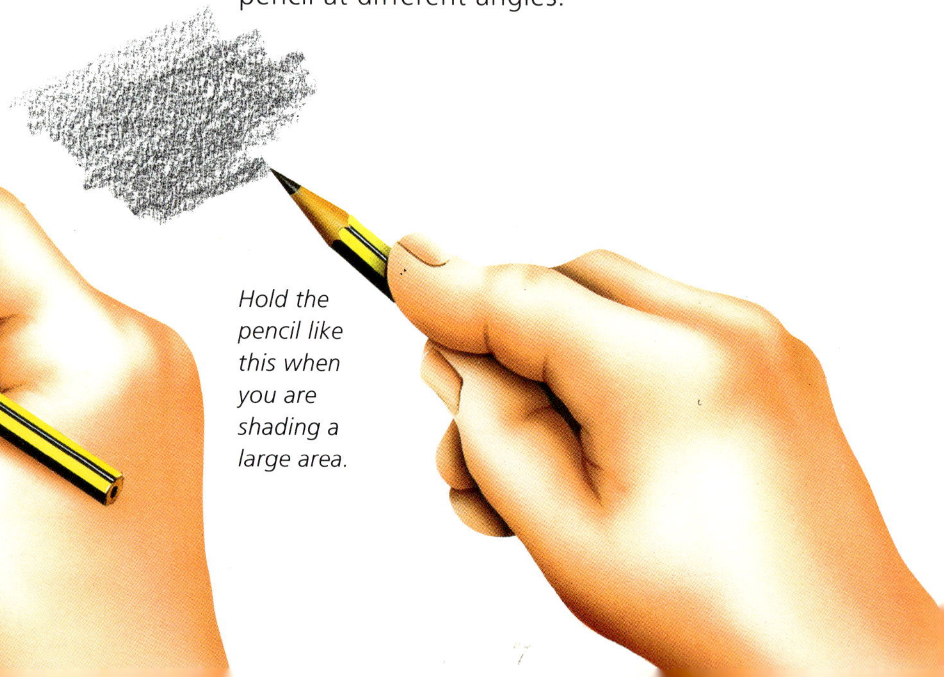

Hold the pencil like this when you are shading a large area.

Drawing skills

Drawing lines

Start with the easiest lines. Here are some basic rules:

- Draw each line once only, without lifting the pencil off the paper. Each line should be continuous, with no breaks
- Don't press too hard on the paper. Use a soft pencil for deep tones
- The lines should look clean and precise. Don't try to go over them or retouch them in any way

Types of lines

Practise drawing different types of lines: short and long lines, straight and curved ones, thick and thin ones, and so on.

The technique is the same for all types of line: only draw it once, draw it firmly and without breaks, and, above all, practise often.

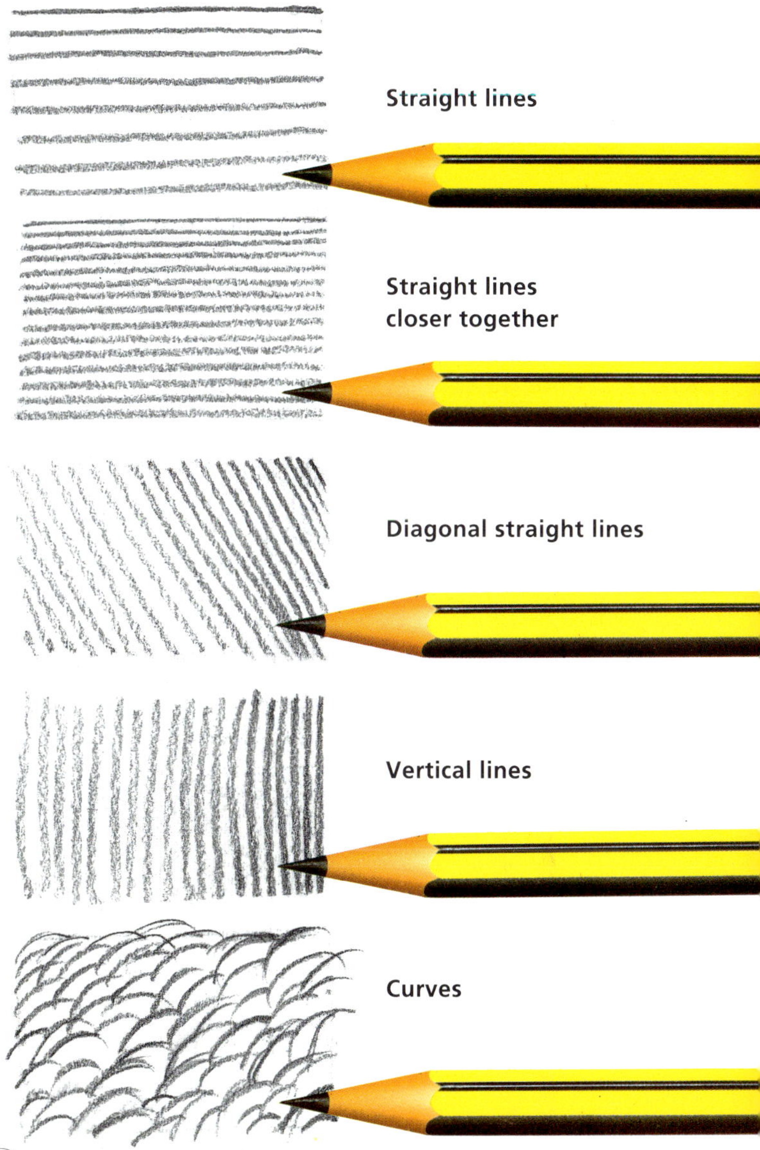

Drawing skills

Shading

Shading is done by drawing lines to make an even tone.

Draw a rectangle and shade it with diagonal lines using a 2B pencil. Make sure the lines are continuous and go in one direction (from left to right). Press evenly on the paper with each stroke.

How to gradate

Use a 2B pencil for your first gradation. Start by drawing a rectangle and draw lines across it with a 2B pencil. Press hard to begin with, and gradually reduce the pressure until the pencil hardly touches the paper.

Go on to try a gradation starting with a medium pencil, such as an HB, and finishing with a soft 2B pencil.

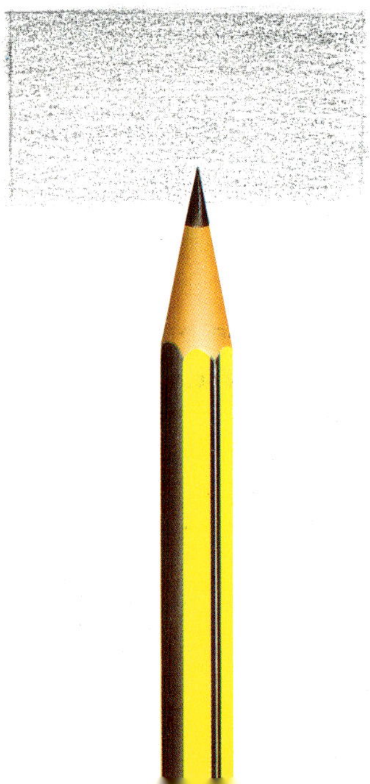

Left: shading an even tone. Always draw the lines in the same direction, and press evenly on the pencil.

Right: how to gradate with two different types of pencil. **1***: a simple gradation with an HB pencil.* **2***: blending with a 2B pencil where the shaded area is paler.*

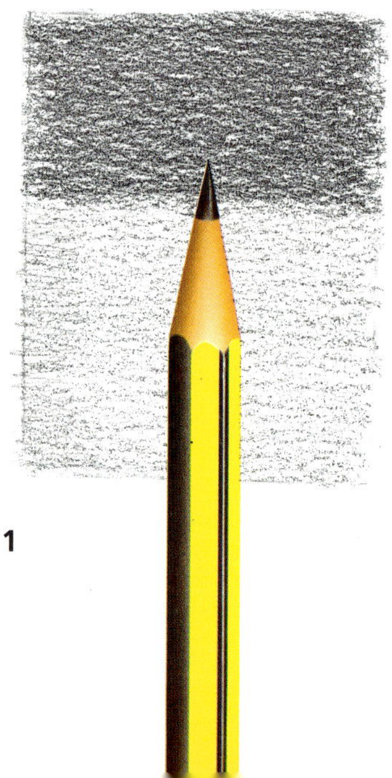

1

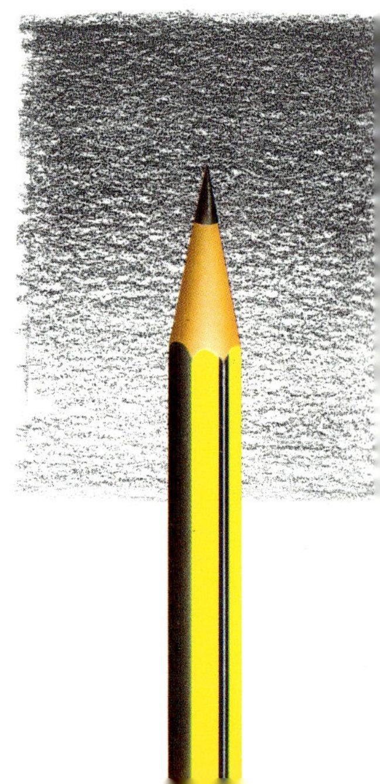

2

Shading with your fingers

You can also use your fingers for shading. To do this you rub the tip of your finger over the pencil lines you have drawn. Press softly and evenly on the paper.

Using a paper stump

Use a paper stump in the same way to shade and gradate. Press very softly on the paper with the stump. Move the paper stump in the same direction as you have drawn the pencil lines - horizontally, vertically, or in curves.

Drawing with a rubber

You can draw with a rubber by rubbing out an area of a picture where you want to make a highlight.

Rub gently over the chosen spot with the rubber.

This page illustrates different ways of making gradations, as well as how to create highlights on a picture.

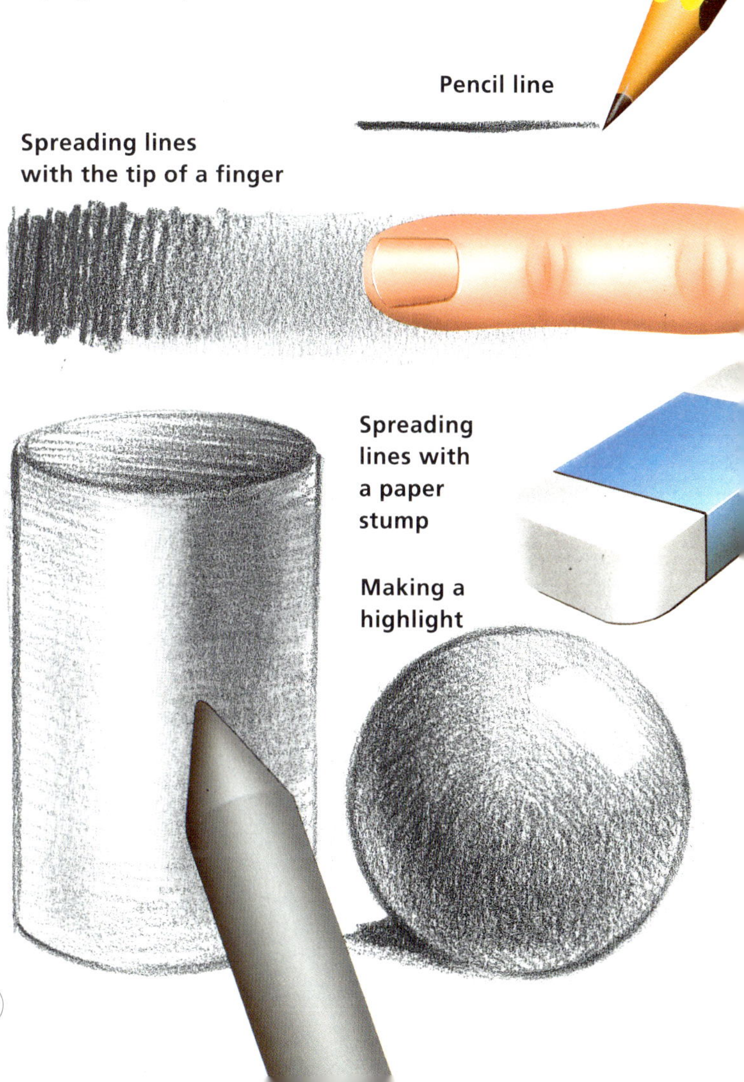

Drawing skills

Making a variety of pencil lines

Charcoal is not suitable for drawing thin lines. You can sharpen it and use the edge of the tip to draw fairly thin lines, but the point will not last very long.

You can draw thicker lines with the angled edge of the tip. If you place the charcoal flat on the paper you can draw very thick lines, ideal for shading or gradating.

To gradate with a lead pencil vary how hard you press with the pencil so that you create different shades of grey.

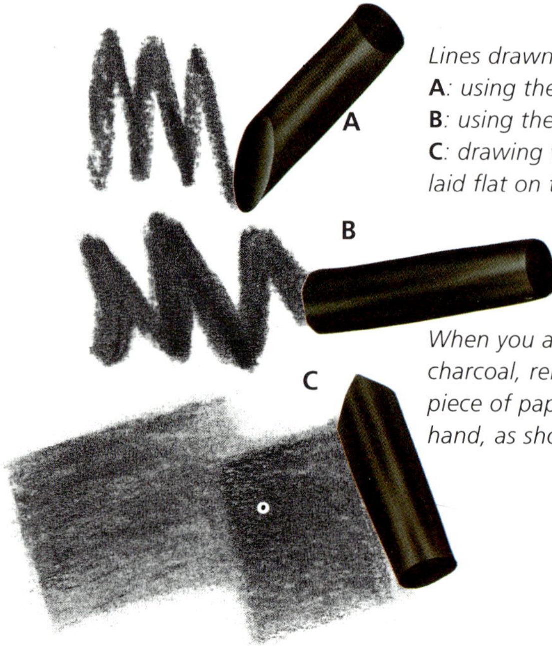

Lines drawn with charcoal.
A: *using the edge of the tip.*
B: *using the flat edge.*
C: *drawing with the charcoal laid flat on the paper.*

When you are drawing with charcoal, remember to put a piece of paper under your hand, as shown below.

Protecting your picture

It is important to protect your picture when you are drawing, especially when you are using charcoal.

Always work with a piece of paper under your hand, so that you don't smudge the picture. Change the piece of paper when it becomes dirty.

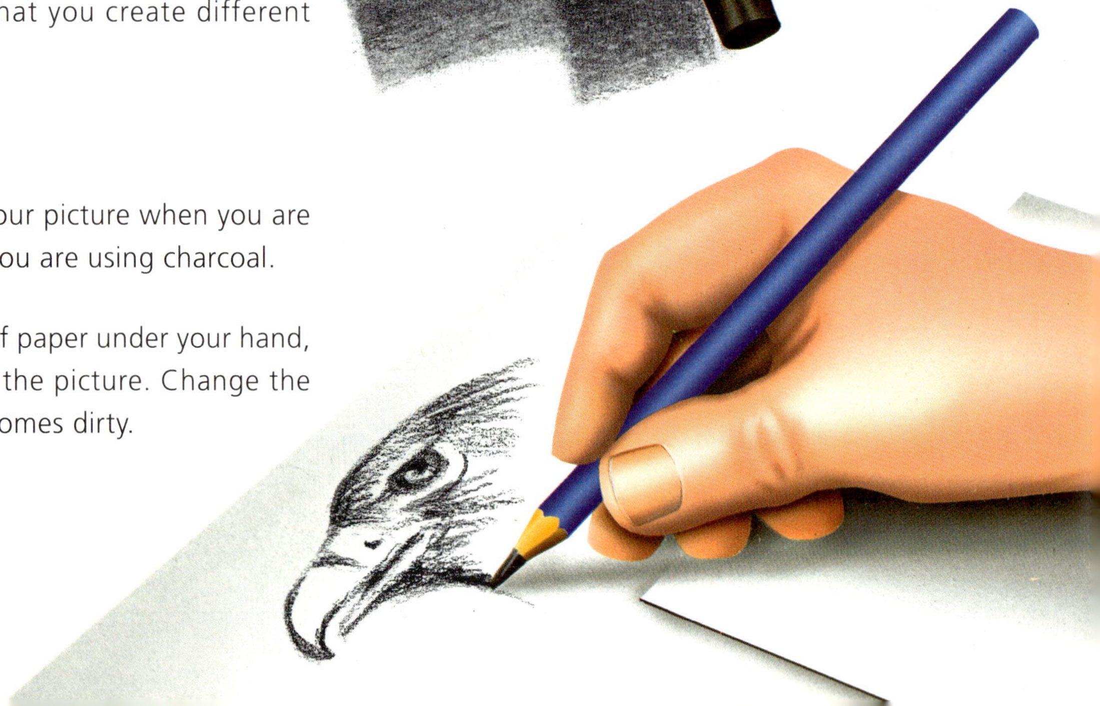

Carbon pencils

Although similiar to charcoal sticks, carbon pencils have their own characteristics:

- Carbon pencil sticks to the paper better
- It is difficult to rub out - you can lighten the tone, but you can't create a white highlight as you can when you rub out lead pencil

When you have finished a picture using either charcoal sticks or a carbon pencil you should fix it. You can buy liquid fixative from any good art shop.

Rubbing out

You can use a rubber or a cloth to remove some lines from the paper, but it is very difficult to rub out lines completely. Use the rubber, or better still your finger, to lighten the tone.

Gradating with carbon pencils

When you try gradating with a carbon pencil, you will find that it goes very dark. You need to draw fewer lines than you would with a lead pencil, and then extend them later on.

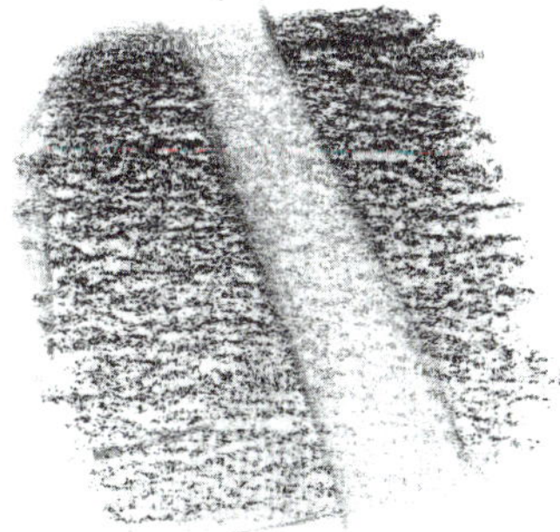
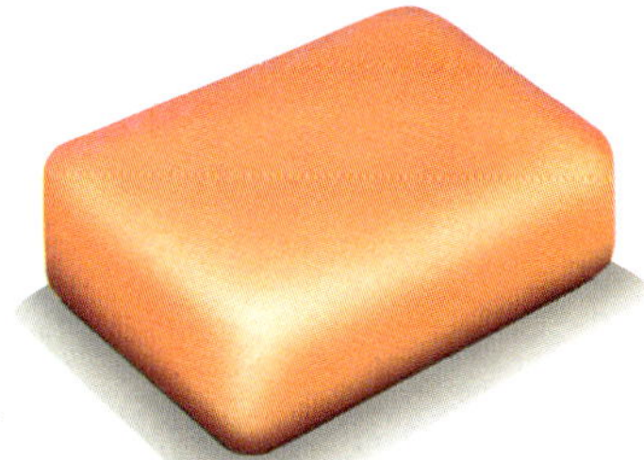

Lines drawn with a carbon pencil

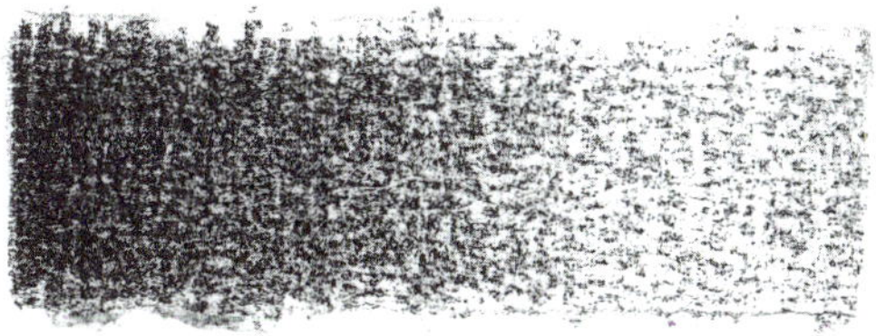

A very long shaded area

This results in a badly-done gradation

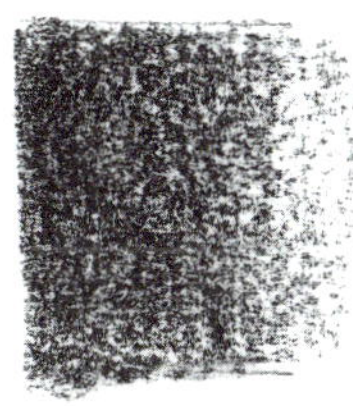

A small shaded area

To gradate well with charcoal or carbon pencil you need to draw fewer lines.

A good gradation

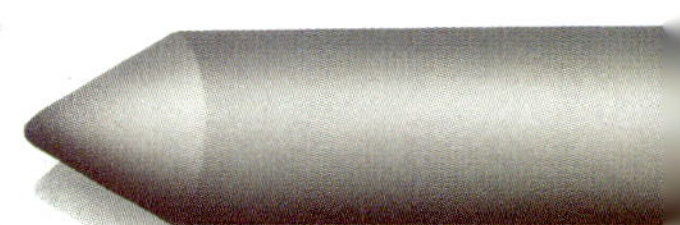

Drawing skills

Dimensions and proportions

When you draw a subject such as a landscape or a figure, you need to transfer the subject's measurements on to paper. The drawing should be a smaller-scale version of the subject on paper.

The best way to do this is to look carefully at the subject before you start drawing and think about its dimensions. How high is it? How wide is it? And so on.

This becomes easier with practice. You can measure dimensions in the following way. Hold a pencil in your hand, and stretch out your arm towards the subject. Line up one end of the pencil with the edge of the subject, and move your thumb along the pencil until it is in line with the other end. Do this to calculate all the dimensions - width,length and height - of your subject.

By calculating dimensions you will be able to draw an accurate sketch. Here, the height of the jug is the same as the width of the jug and the apple together, and the apple's width is the same as the top of the jug.

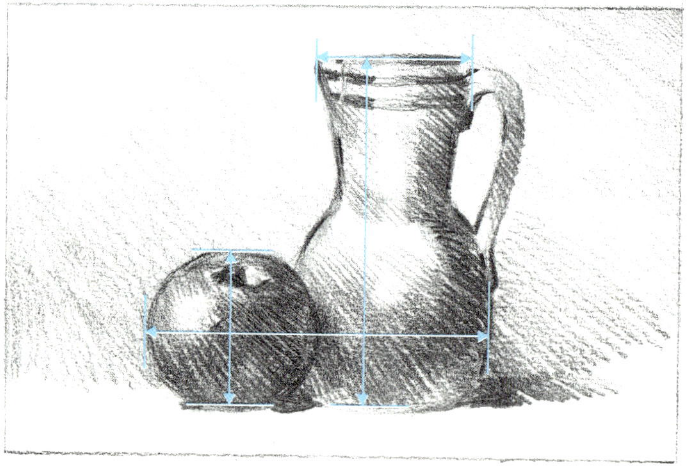

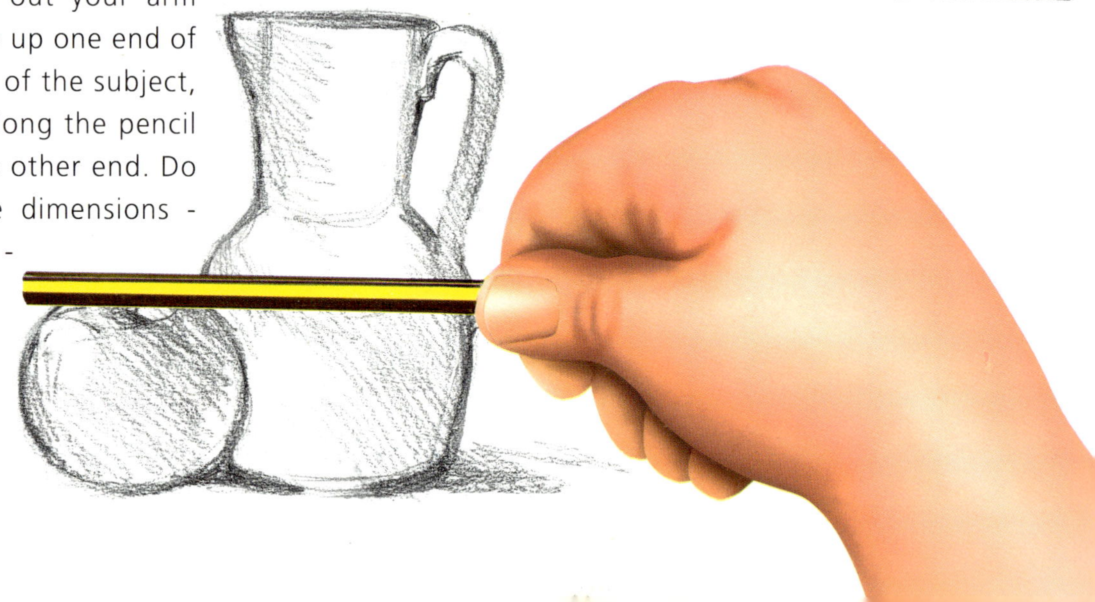

Drawing skills

Drawing with a grid

If you want to copy a picture exactly, you can draw a grid over the top of it, then draw another grid with the same number of squares on a piece of paper.

Copy the picture square by square on´to the blank grid.

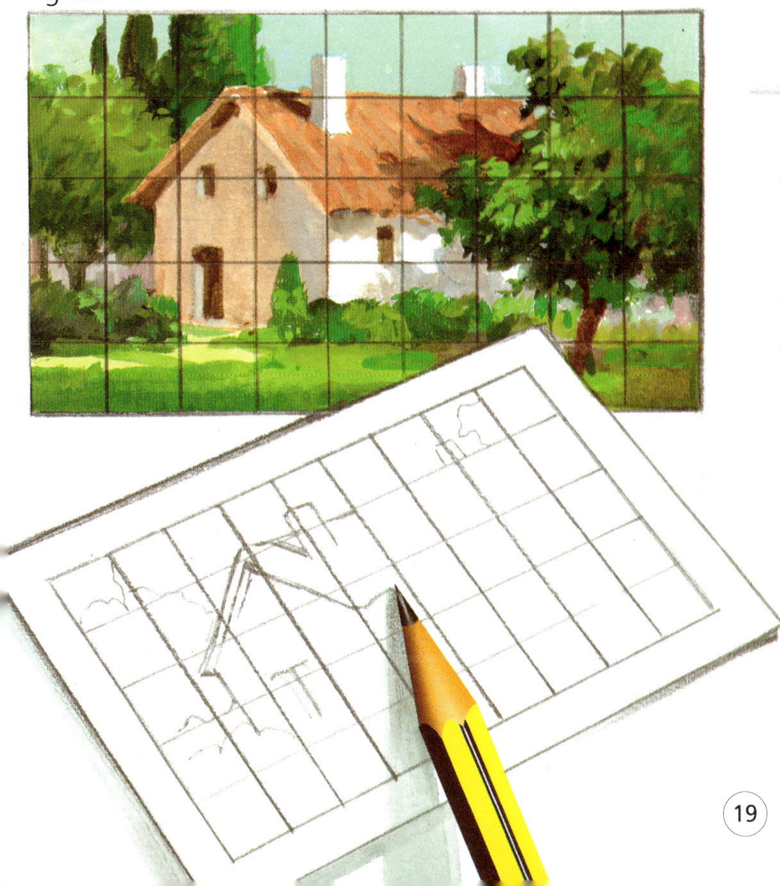

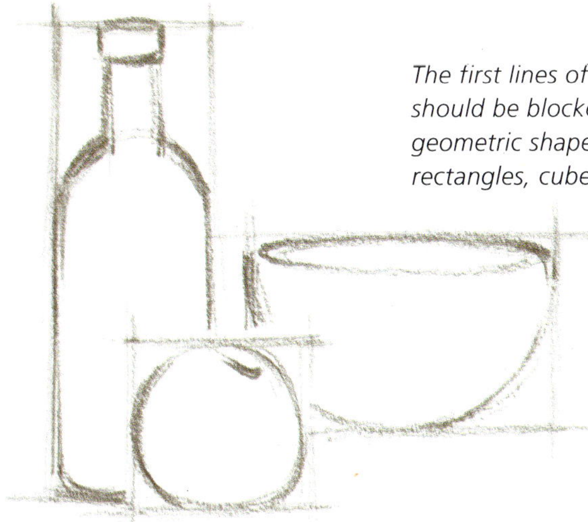

The first lines of a picture should be blocked in as geometric shapes - squares, rectangles, cubes, etc.

Blocking in

Always begin a drawing by blocking in. This means drawing geometric shapes to represent the main elements in your picture.

Geometric shapes are never exactly the same as the shapes of your subject, so the idea of blocking in is to give you a rough guide when starting a picture. Look at the two examples on this page, then look at other objects and try to imagine which geometric shapes you could use to block them in.

Drawing skills

What is perspective?

Pictures are drawn on paper, a flat surface which has two dimensions: width and height. But objects have a third dimension, or depth.

The rules of perspective help you to show the depth or third dimension of your subject on the flat surface of the paper.

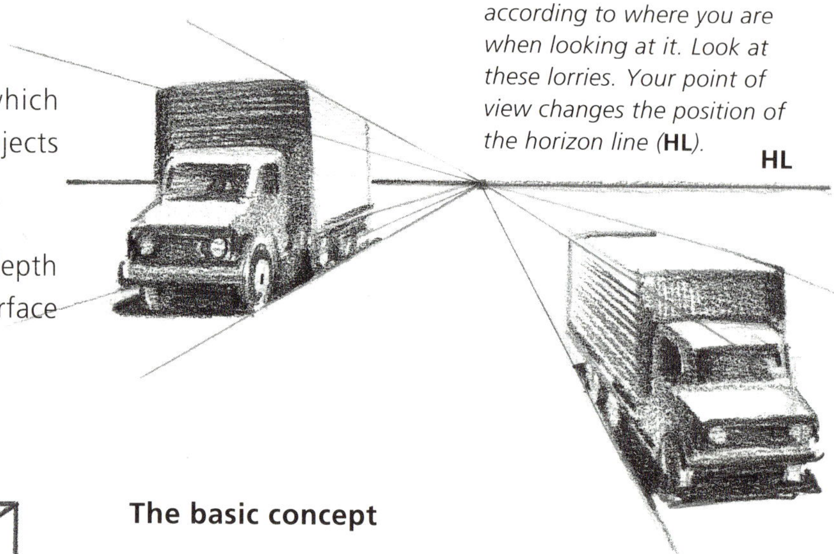

*Your view of a subject varies according to where you are when looking at it. Look at these lorries. Your point of view changes the position of the horizon line (**HL**).*

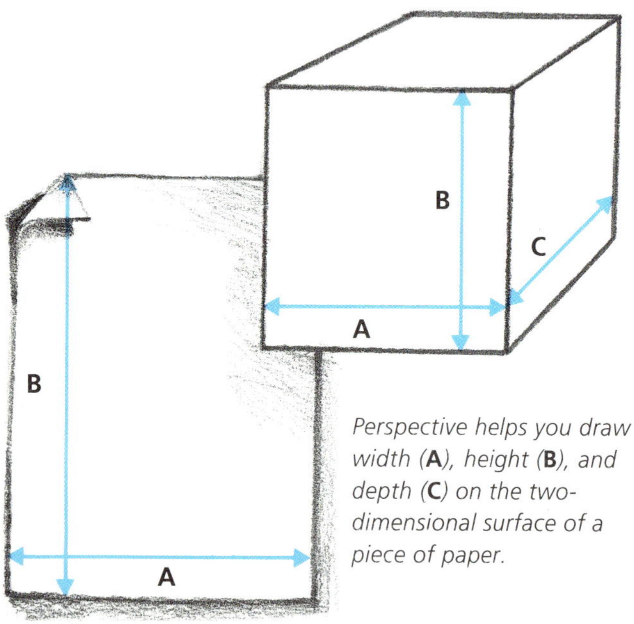

*Perspective helps you draw width (**A**), height (**B**), and depth (**C**) on the two-dimensional surface of a piece of paper.*

The basic concept

Perspective is complicated, but well worth mastering. There are a few basic rules to bear in mind when you are drawing pictures.

Imagine that you are looking at a house. You could position yourself directly in front of the house, or you could move to the right or left of it. The place where you are standing is called the point of view (PV).

Another term used in perspective is the horizon line (HL). The position of this line varies according to your point of view. Look at the illustrations on these pages and read the captions next to them.

Types of perspective

There are three types of perspective:

- ○ Parallel perspective, with one vanishing point
- ○ Oblique perspective, with two vanishing points
- ○ Aerial perspective, with three vanishing points

The vanishing point is on the horizon; it is the place where the lines used to draw perspective meet. With parallel and oblique perspective the vertical lines of a drawing are always parallel to each other, while the rest of the lines (all the horizontal ones) meet at the vanishing point(s).

These are the two types of perspective you will use most in your drawings. Aerial perspective is used when you are looking at a building from above or below. The vertical lines in aerial perspective meet at a third vanishing point.

Practising with geometric shapes

Practise drawing the shapes here. It is easier to see how perspective works by drawing geometric shapes.

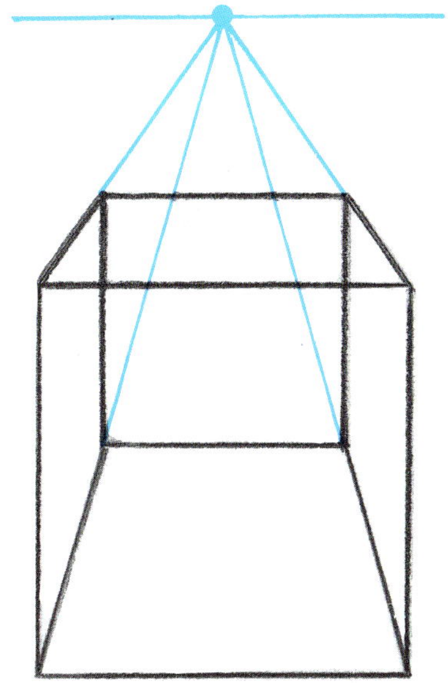

*In parallel perspective the vanishing lines - here the extensions of the cube that will be rubbed out later - meet at only one vanishing point (**VP**).*

Parallel perspective

*In oblique perspective - when you look at something from one side - there are two vanishing points (**VP**).*

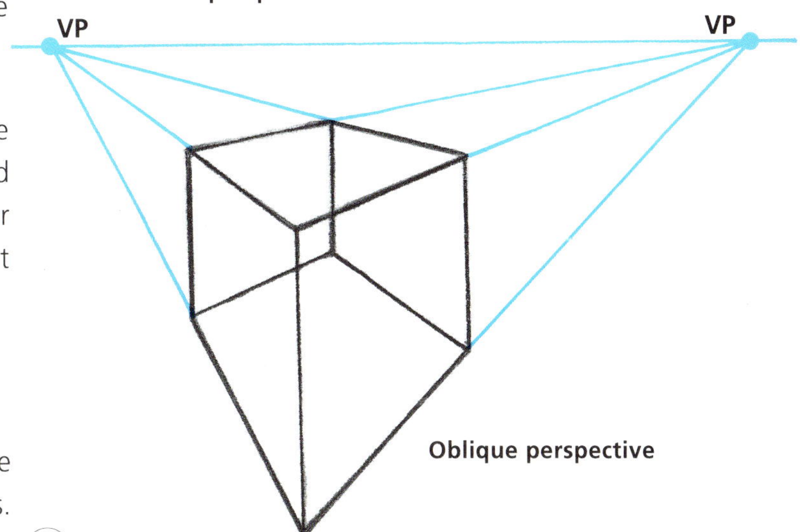

Oblique perspective

First projects

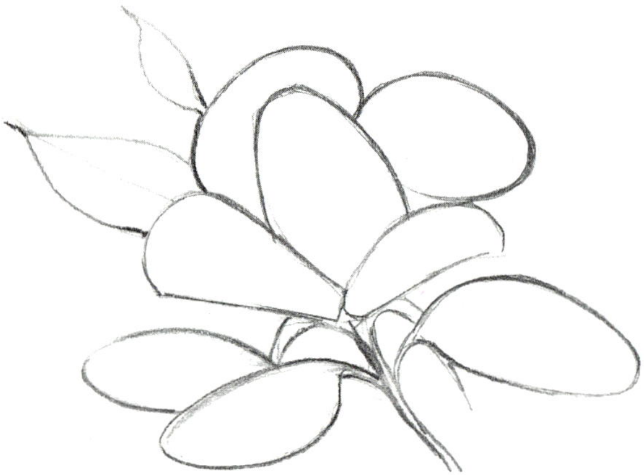

This first drawing gives you practice in blocking in flowers with simple geometric shapes.

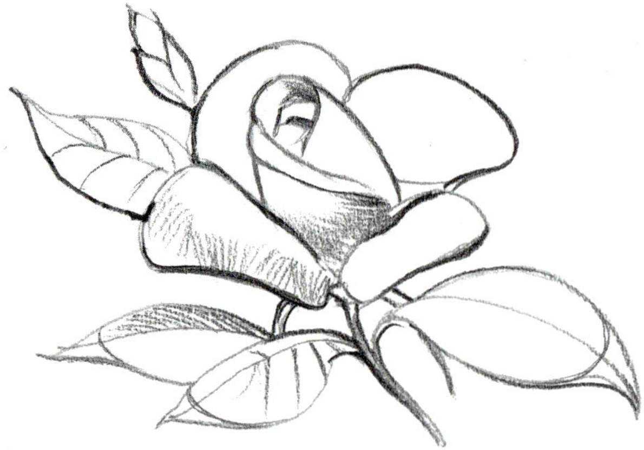

Outline and finish the shapes of the leaves and draw the details of the flower. Then sketch the shadows with parallel lines.

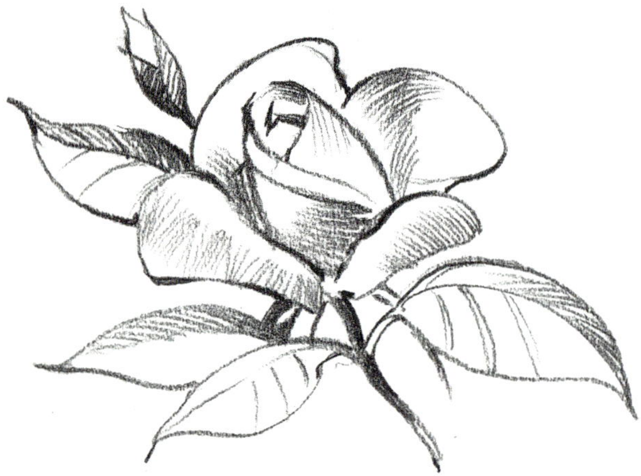

Darken the shadows using parallel lines which follow the horizontal lines of the rose, and vertical lines on the edges of the leaves.

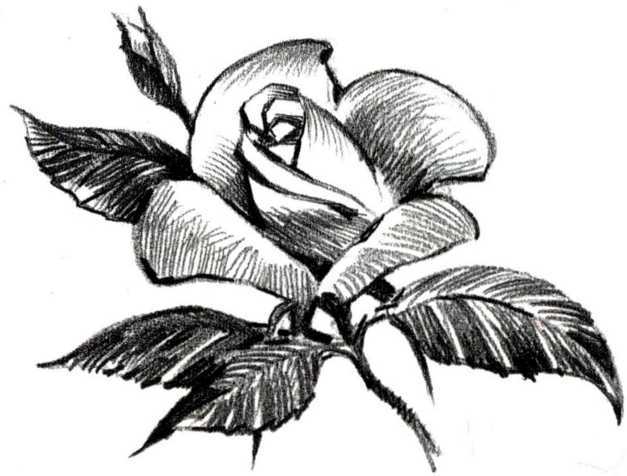

Continue working on the lines. Draw them closer together with a 2B pencil, and create different shades of grey.

First projects

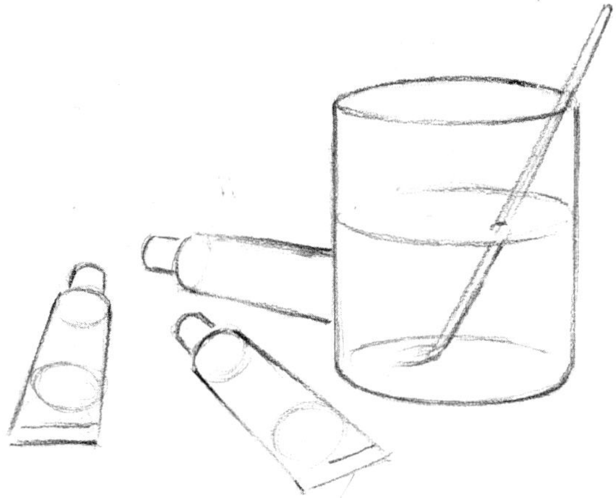

Sketch the objects so that they look three-dimensional. Draw circles to represent the top and bottom of the water jar.

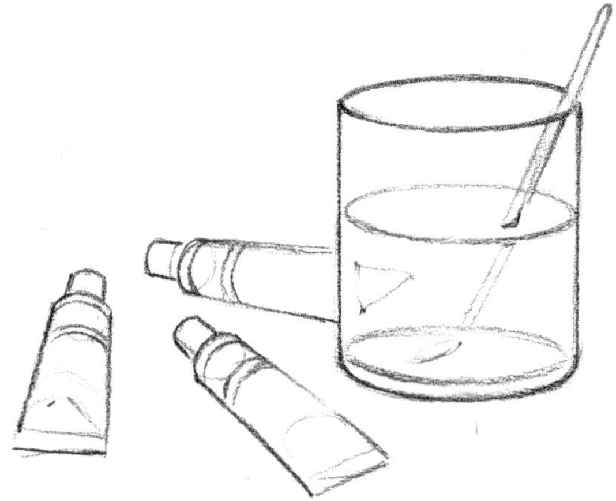

Strengthen the lines of the drawing. Then start to draw in the details of the paint tubes, and mark the highlights on the water jar.

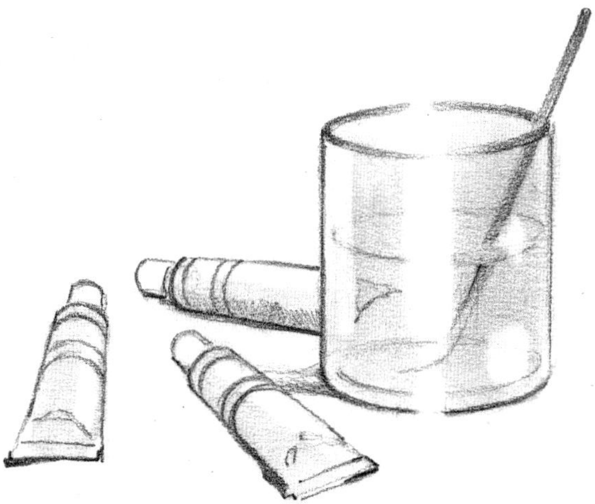

Do some general shading. Don't press too hard with the pencil, and use lines that follow the basic shape of the water jar. Make a highlight in the centre of the water jar with a rubber.

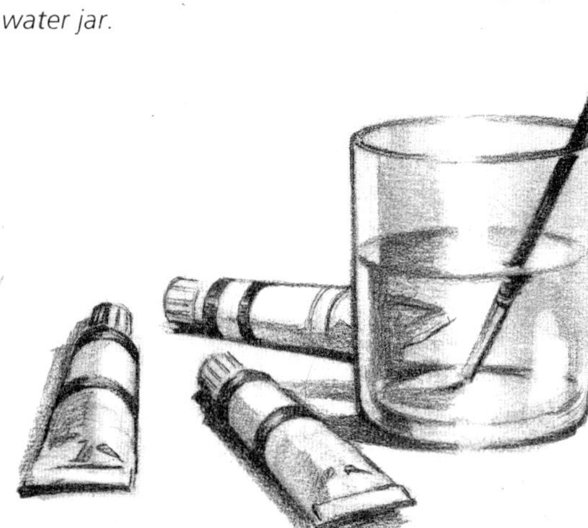

Add darker tones using a soft pencil. Press harder on the pencil in the shadows.

First projects

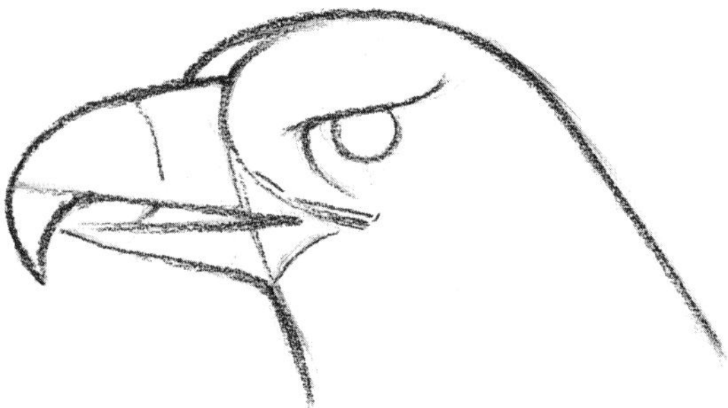

Do this drawing with a charcoal pencil. The shape of the eagle's head is quite simple, and can be drawn with a few basic lines.

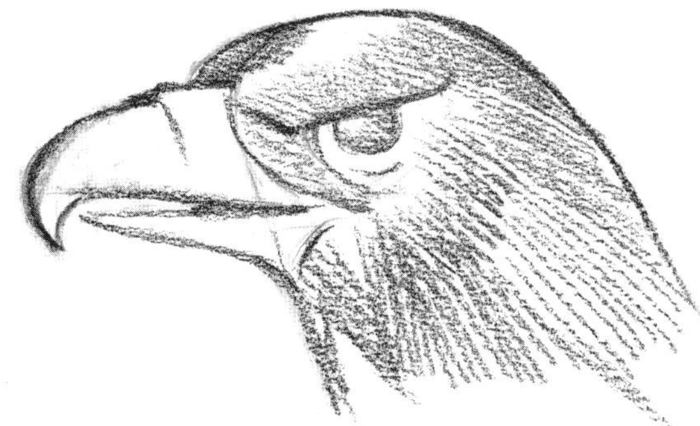

Shade the head with parallel lines, pressing lightly with the pencil. Start by drawing lines going in one direction, then cross them with lines going in the opposite direction. This is how to shade the darker areas.

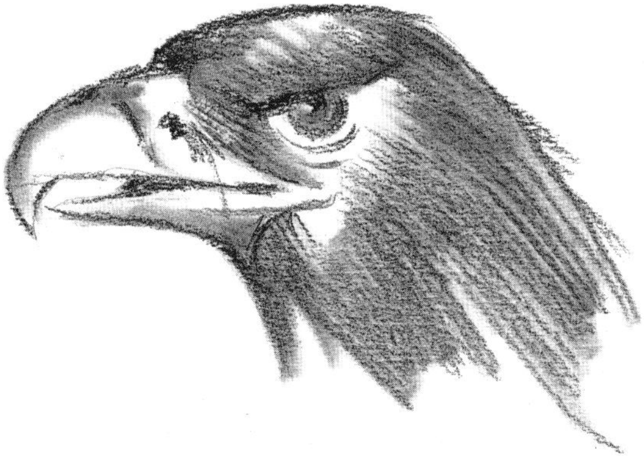

Now smooth the lines with your fingertips or with a paper stump. Do this carefully, as the charcoal spreads very easily. The most important areas are the beak and the upper part of the eye.

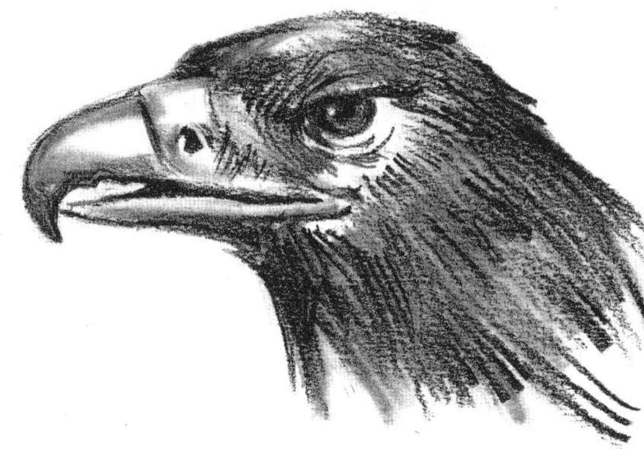

Finally, create some contrast by going over the shadow on the beak, the eye and the plumage once or twice.

First projects

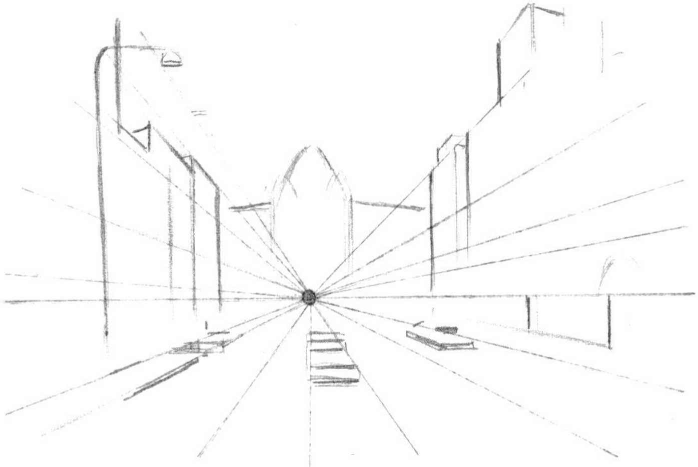

Here is some practice in perspective. Draw the first lines and join them to the vanishing point on the horizon line.

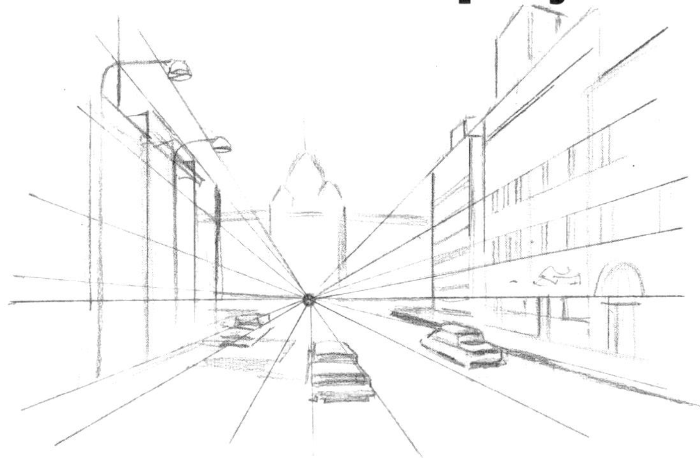

You can use a ruler so that all the horizontal vanishing lines meet in the right place.

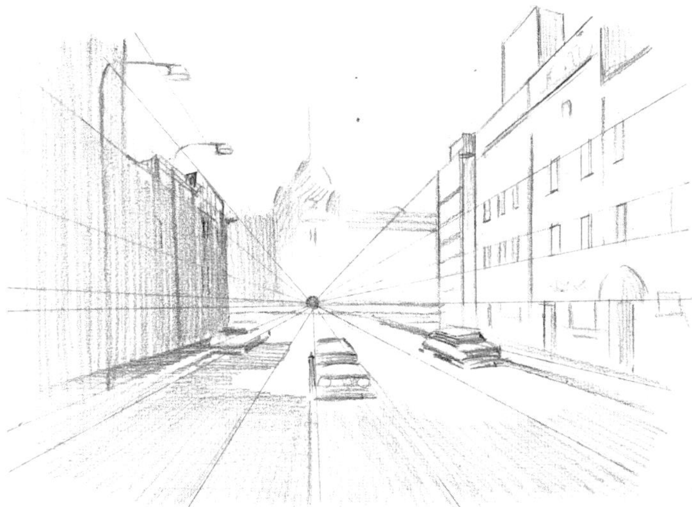

Do some shading, making sure that the lines go in the same direction.

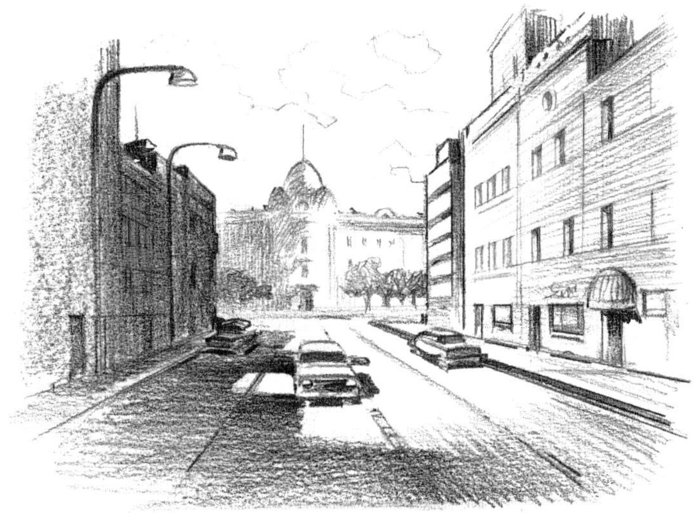

Work a little more on the shadows in the foreground, and soften the background to give the drawing more depth.

Advanced projects

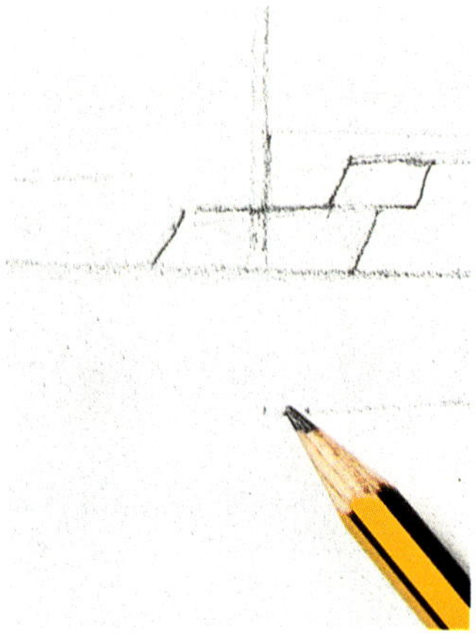

Block in the shape of the boat's hull.

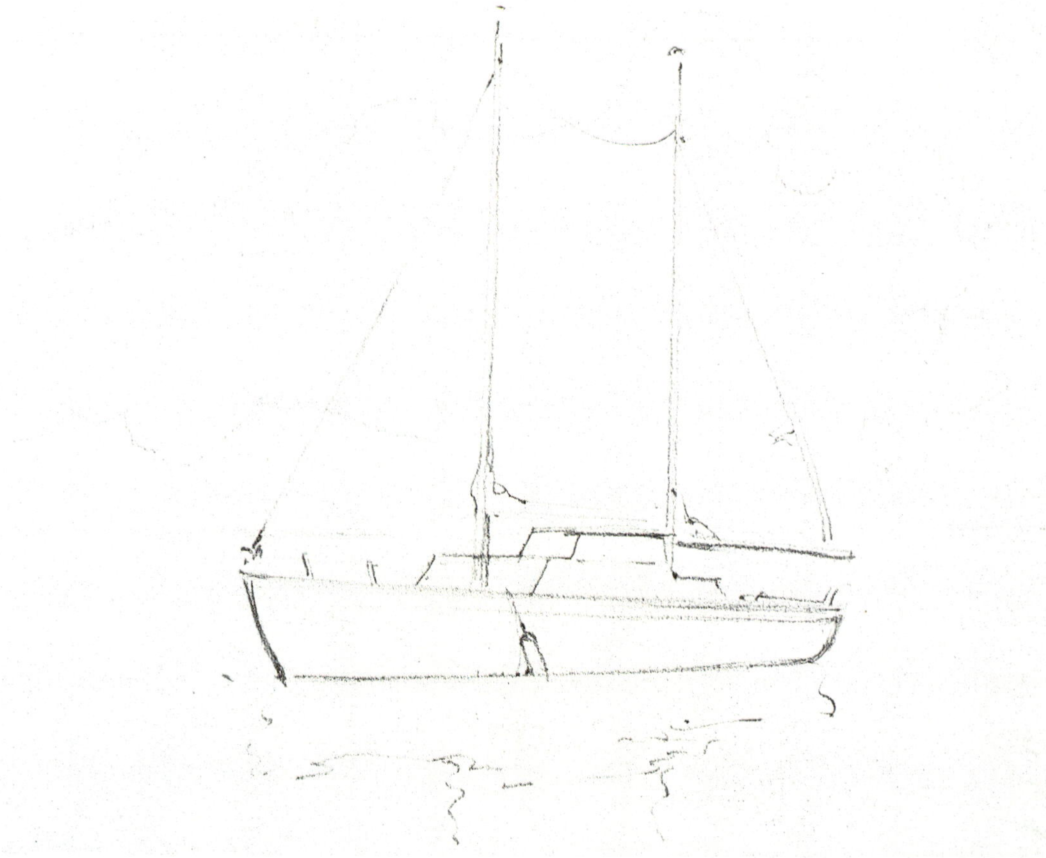

This drawing is done with parallel lines.

Start by drawing the main lines to form the shape of the boat. Put in the horizon line, the clouds and the boat's reflection on the water

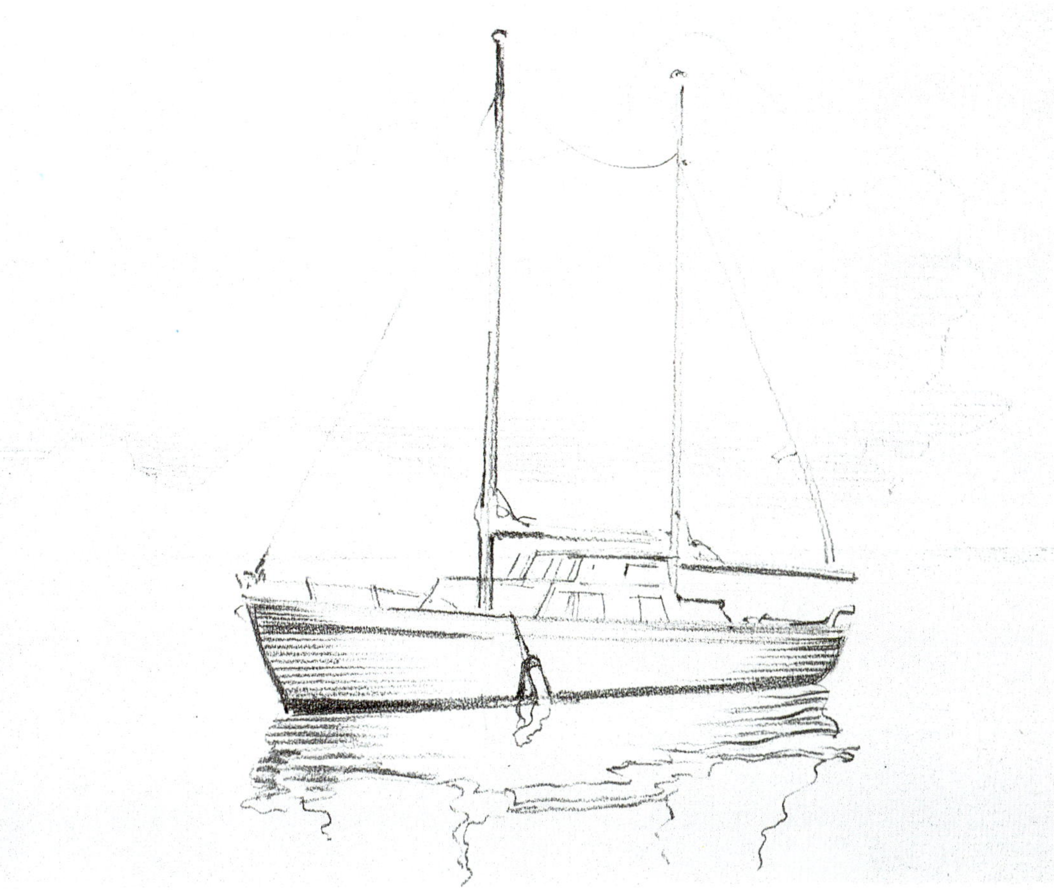

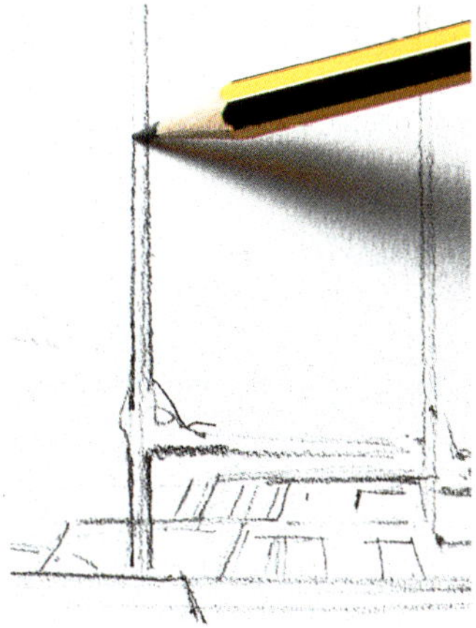

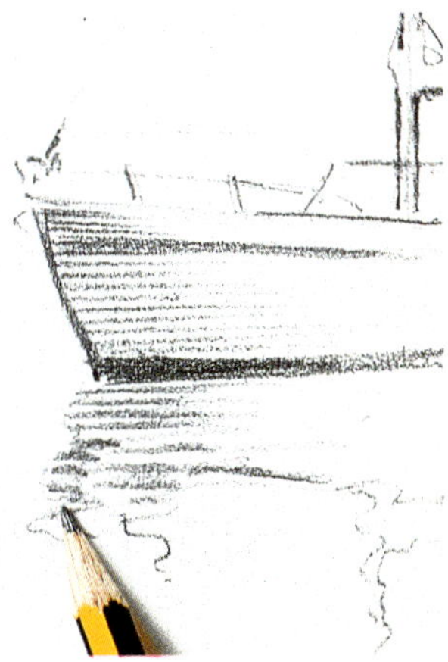

When you have finished your initial sketch, go over the main lines of the drawing, especially the hull and the masts. Now start to draw parallel lines in the clouds. Make them very light by hardly touching the paper with the pencil. To convey the boat's reflections in the water, lightly shade with horizontal pencil strokes.

Advanced projects

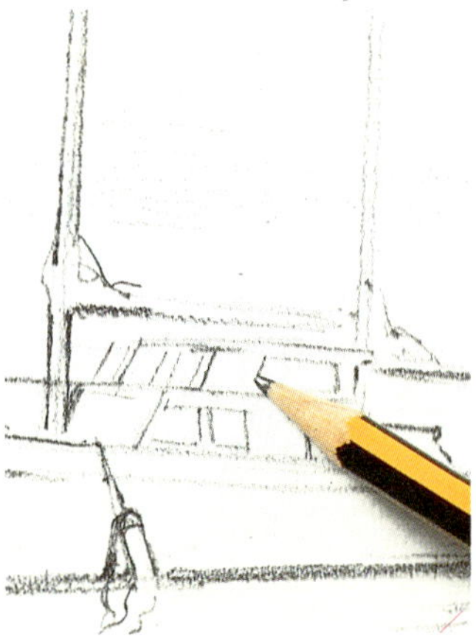

Go over the lines of the drawing and draw in the details, including the windows and cabins.

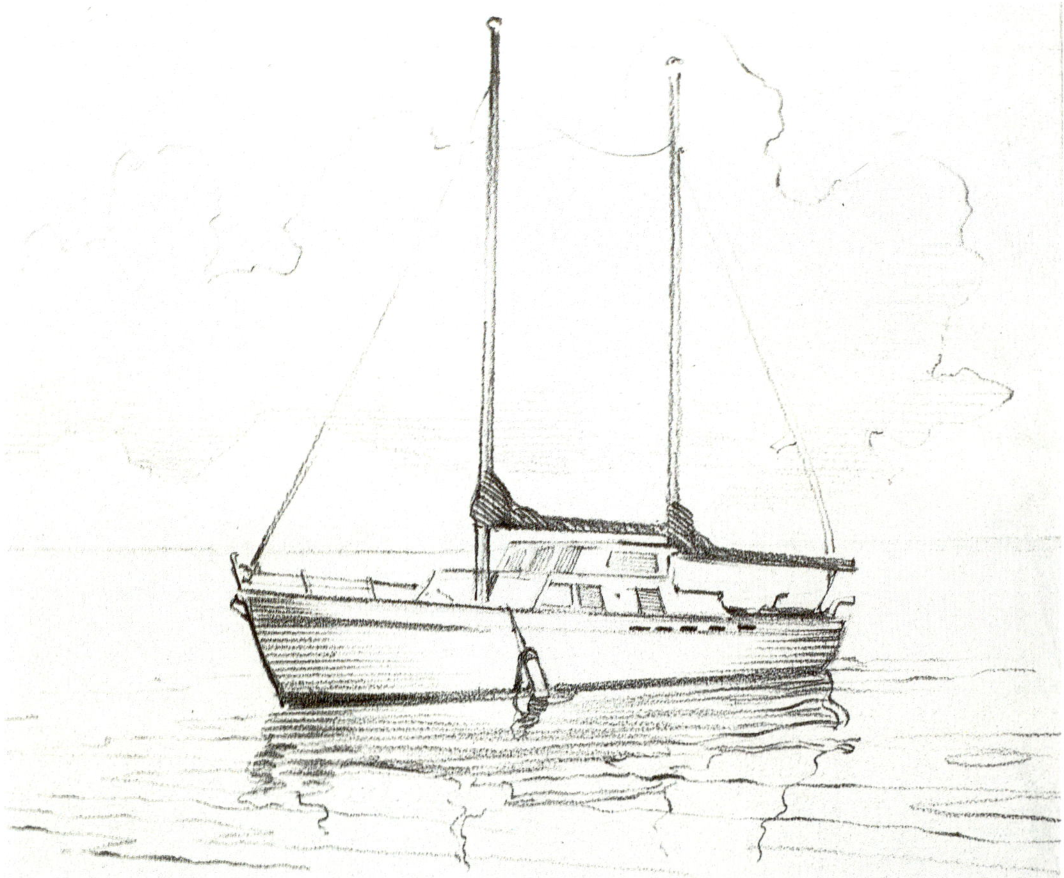

The next stage is to draw very dark parallel lines diagonally across the sails.

Do the same, but more softly, on the cabin windows.

Pressing lightly, draw a few lines in the boat's reflection on the water.

Draw the shapes of the waves at the bottom of the picture.

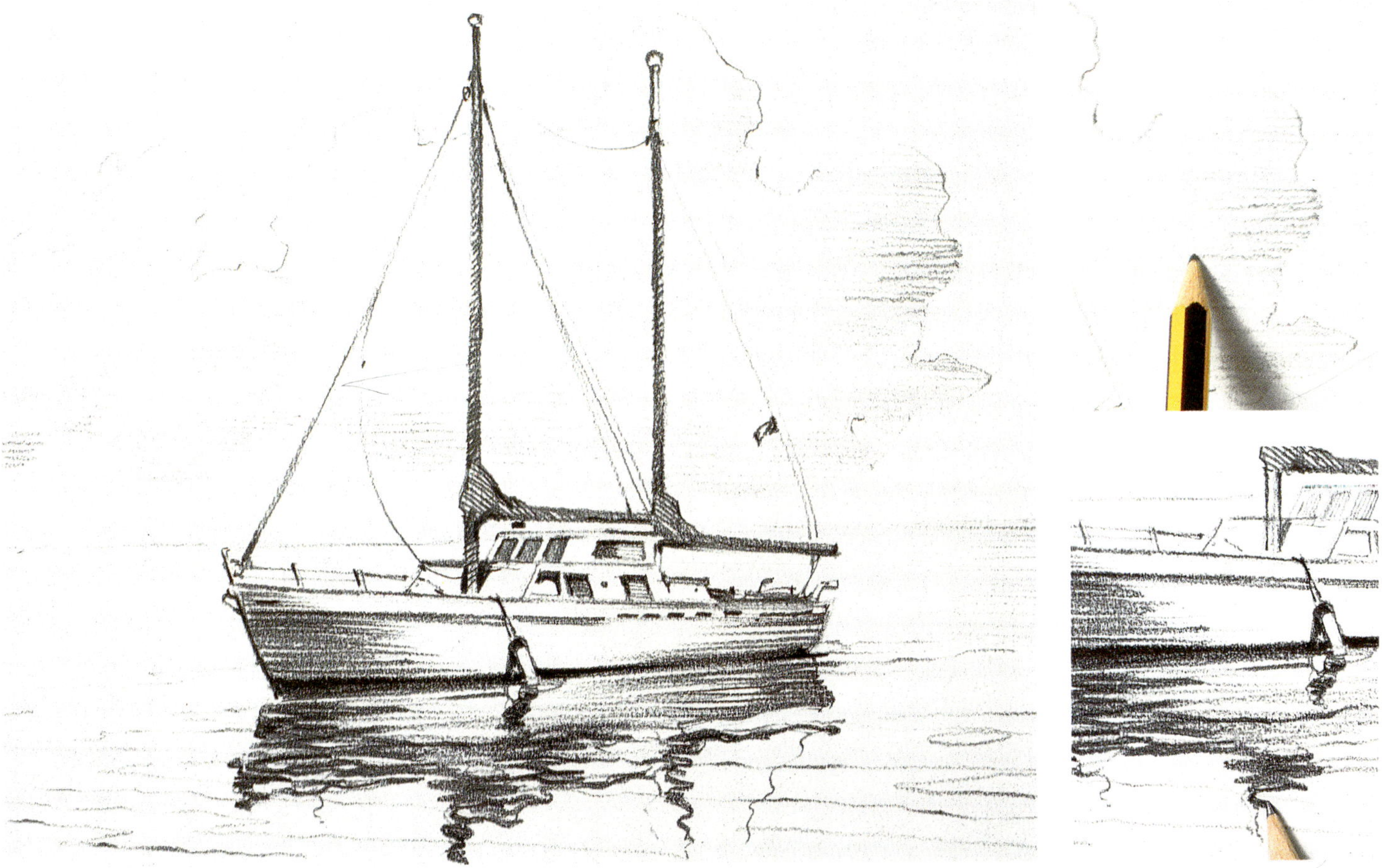

Now you need to darken the tones.

Draw softer lines in the clouds, making sure that you create some darker grey areas by drawing heavier lines.

Do the same for the cabin windows. Draw lines close together in the dark areas and further apart in the lighter ones to create gradations on the boat's hull and the reflections on the water.

Advanced projects

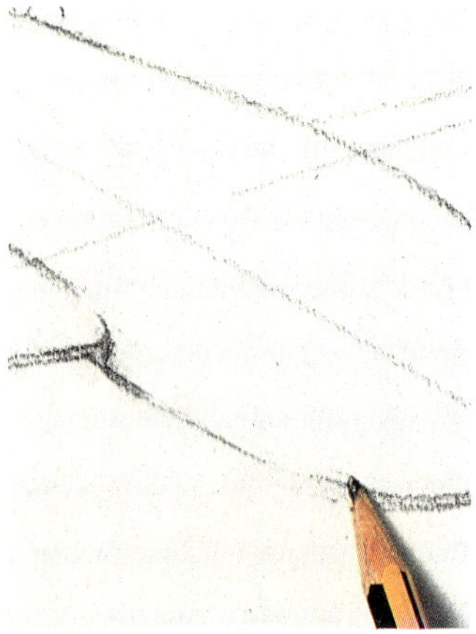

Try to match the basic lines of the sketch with geometric shapes. The plane's fuselage can be blocked in as a cylinder.

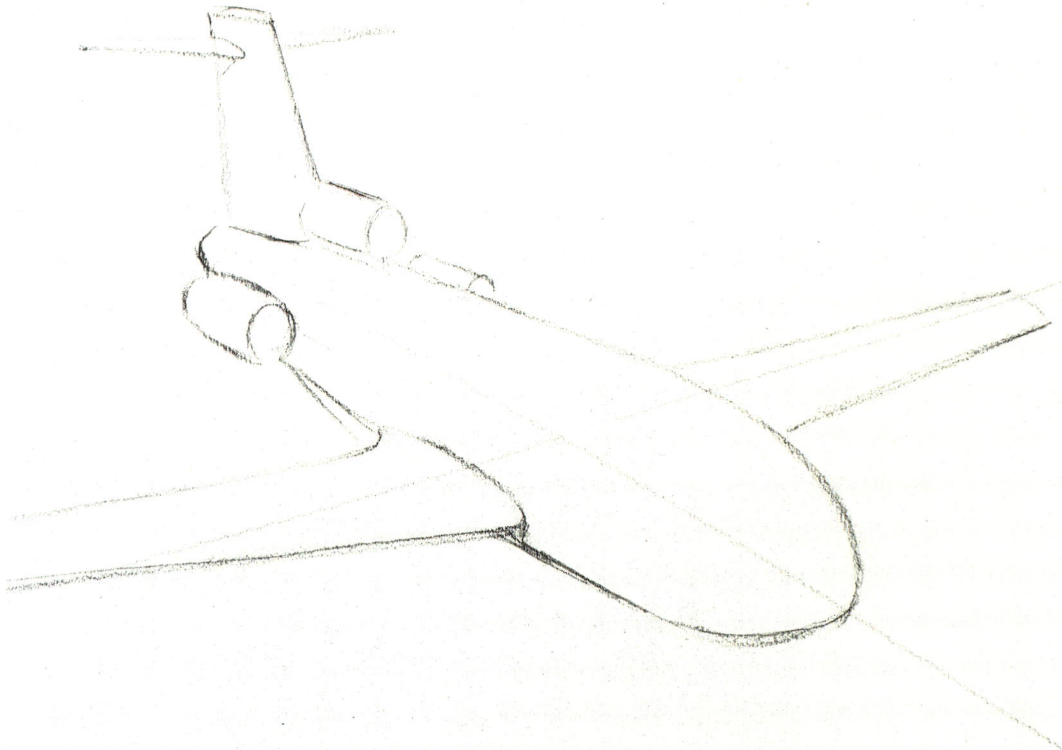

For this project you need to use a lead pencil.

Draw two lines at right angles on the paper, and position the fuselage and wings on them.

Then draw in the main lines with an HB pencil. Like the fuselage, the engines are cylindrical. The wings can be blocked in as triangles.

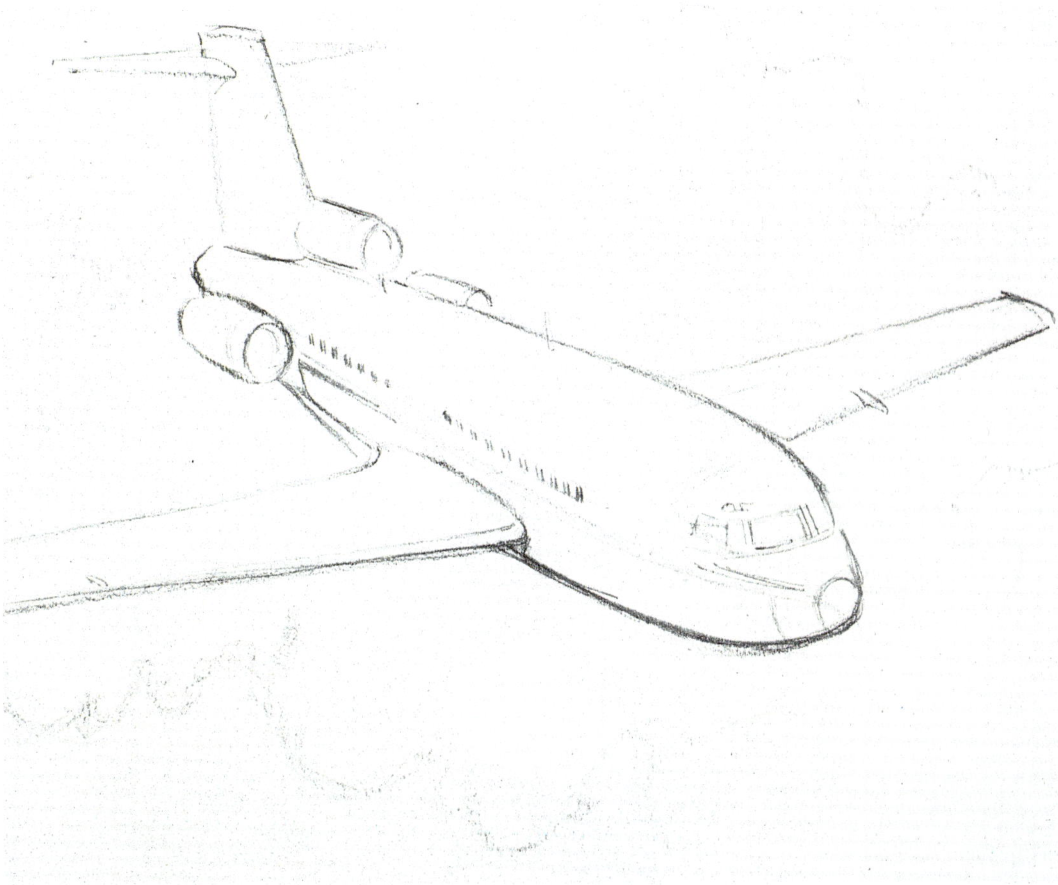

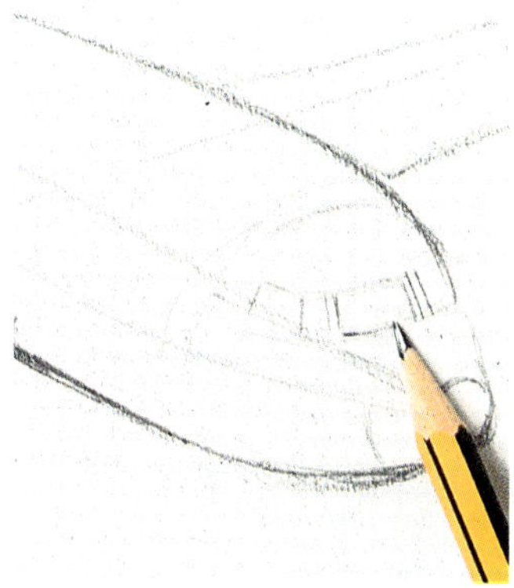

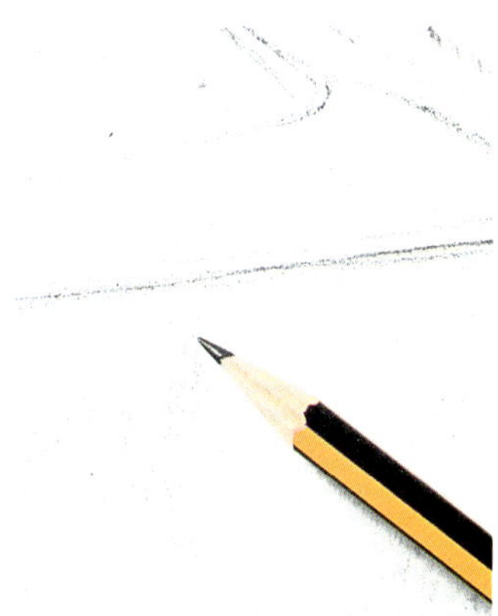

Go over the lines with a 2B pencil to strengthen the shapes of your preliminary sketch.

Start adding details to the drawing.

Draw the windows and define the plane's nose.

Draw in the shapes of the clouds.

Advanced projects

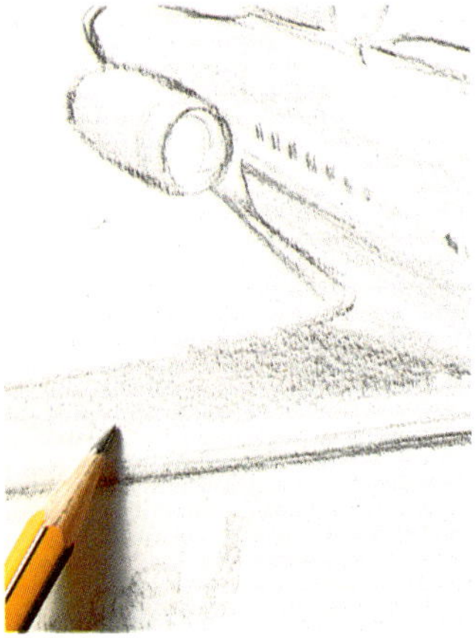

Gradate the shading on the wings as you learned to do earlier, varying the pressure on the pencil.

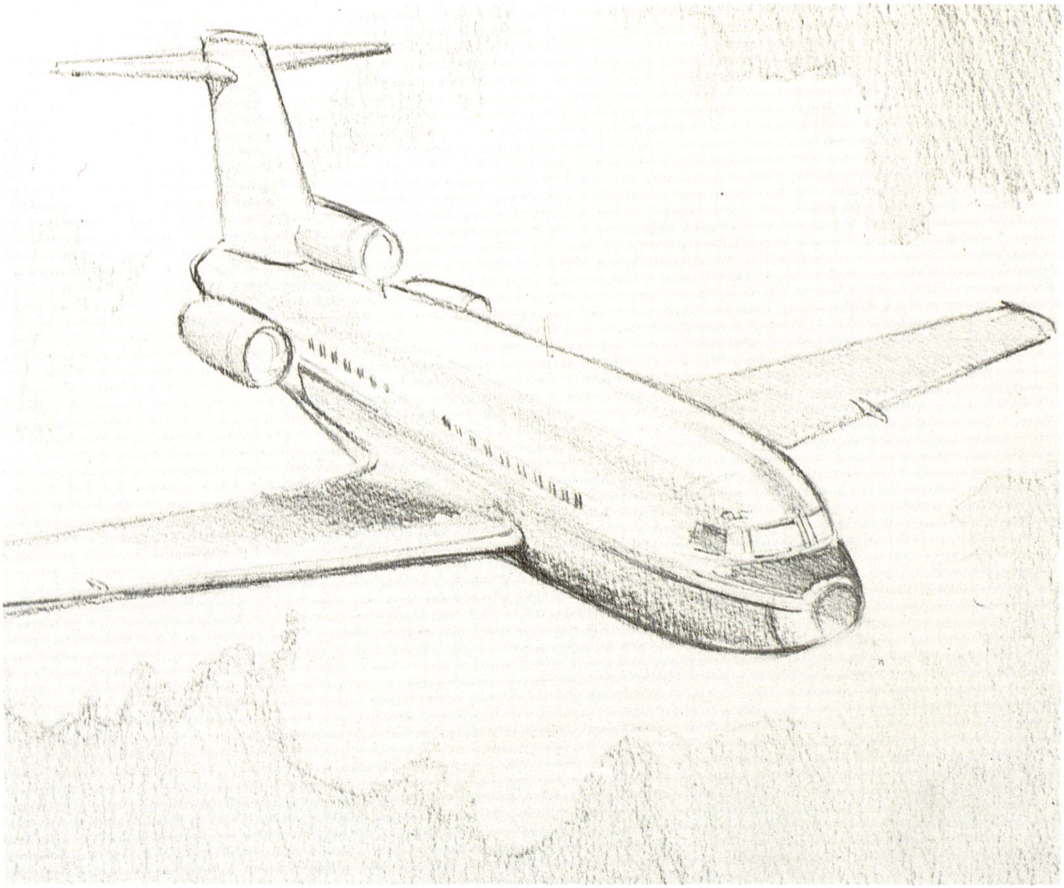

Now work on the shadows.

Hold the pencil in a flat position and cover the background with soft lines, keeping an even pressure on the pencil.

Draw parallel lines on the wings, making the lines closer together on one wing. Do the same on the fuselage, making the nose darker grey.

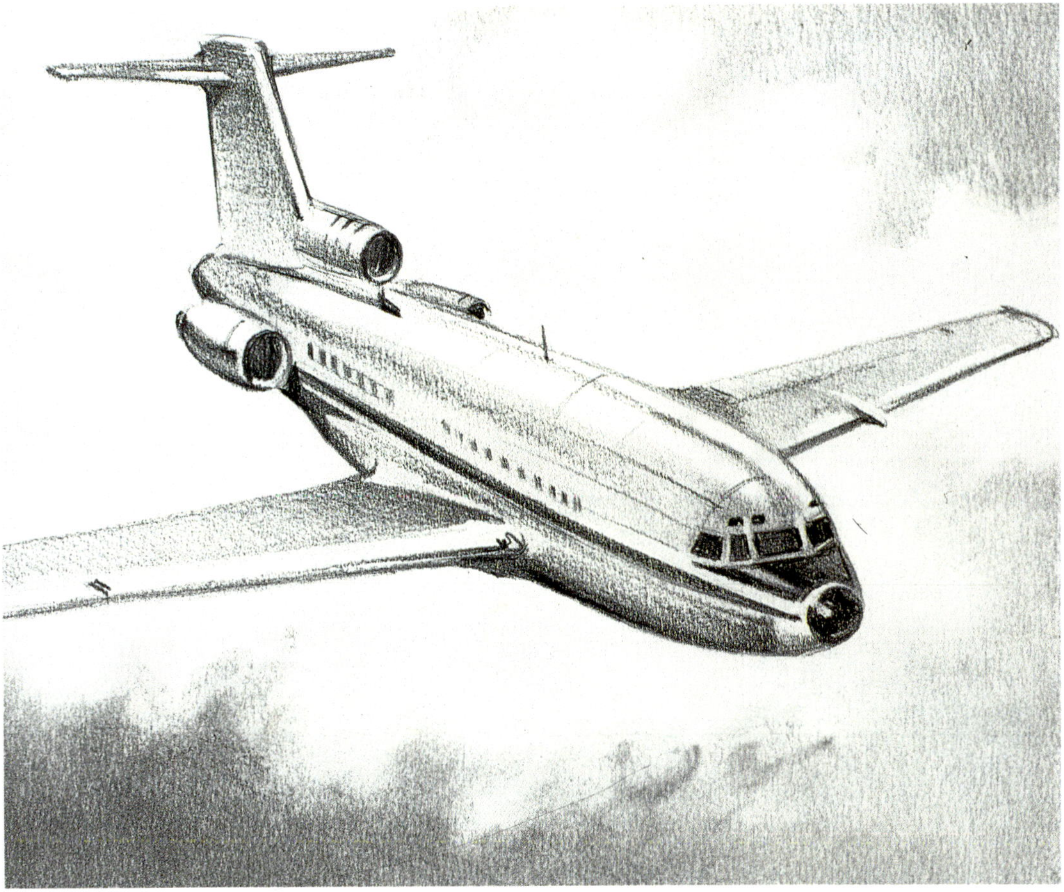

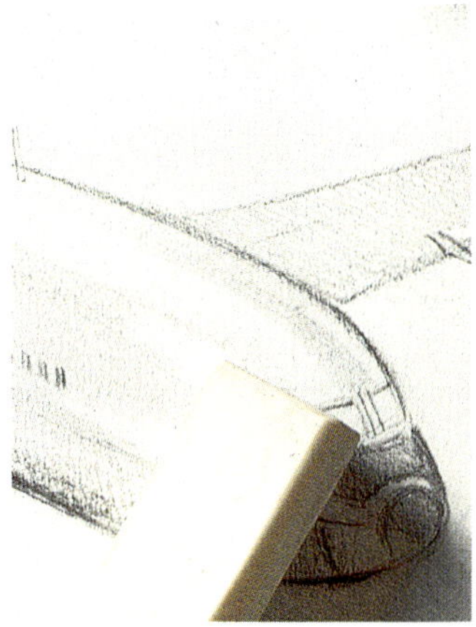

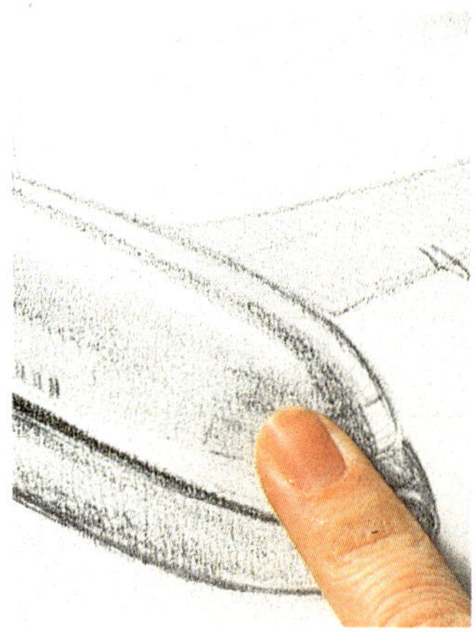

Rub the sky between the clouds with the tip of the paper stump.

Use a 2B pencil to create darker tones on the tail, the engines and the windows.

Make some highlights with a rubber, and even out the shading a little more with your fingertips.

Advanced projects

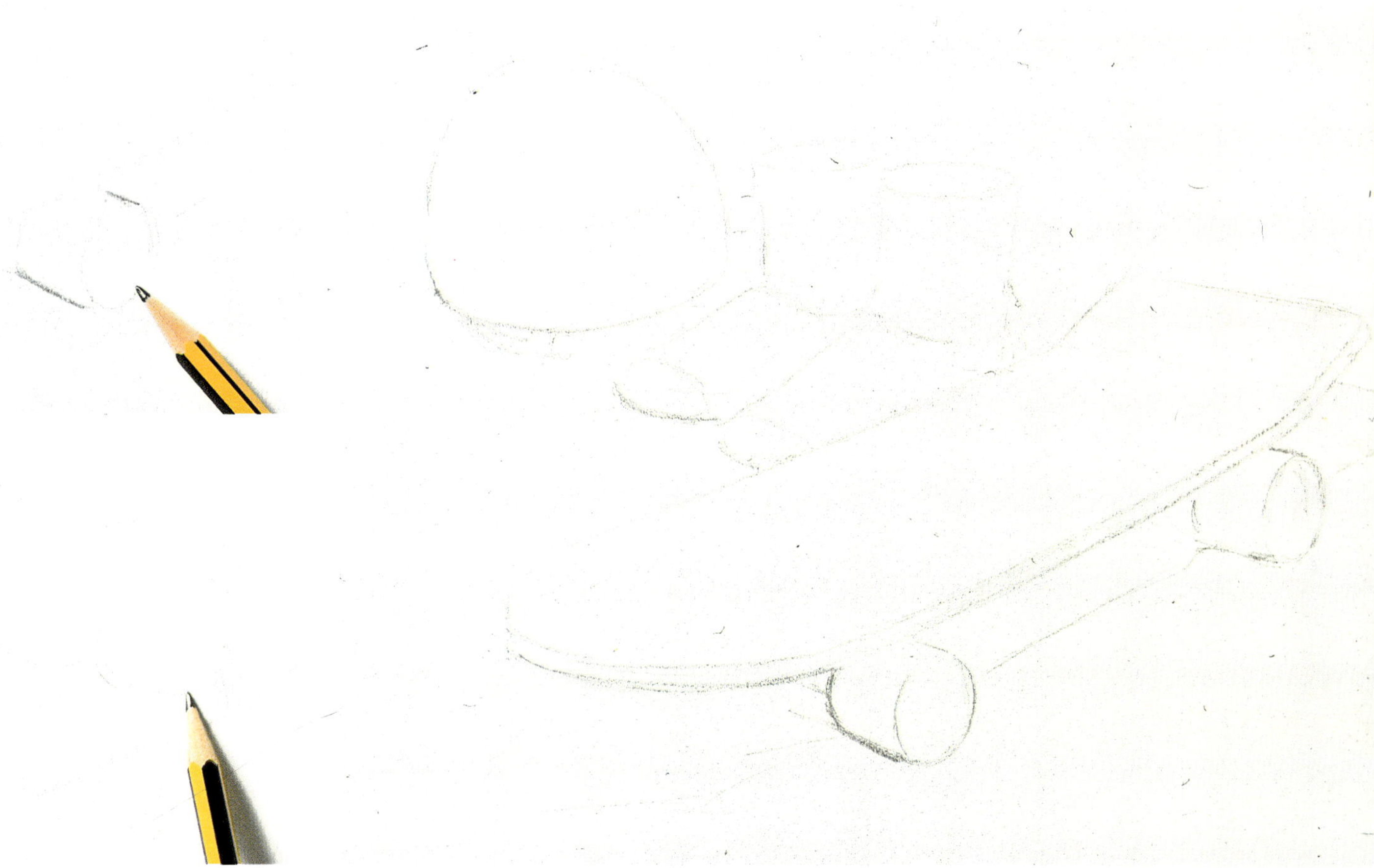

This is a picture to draw with a charcoal pencil. As it is difficult to rub out lines drawn with charcoal, it is a good idea to do your initial sketch with a pencil.

When you have done more drawing, you can try starting off with charcoal.

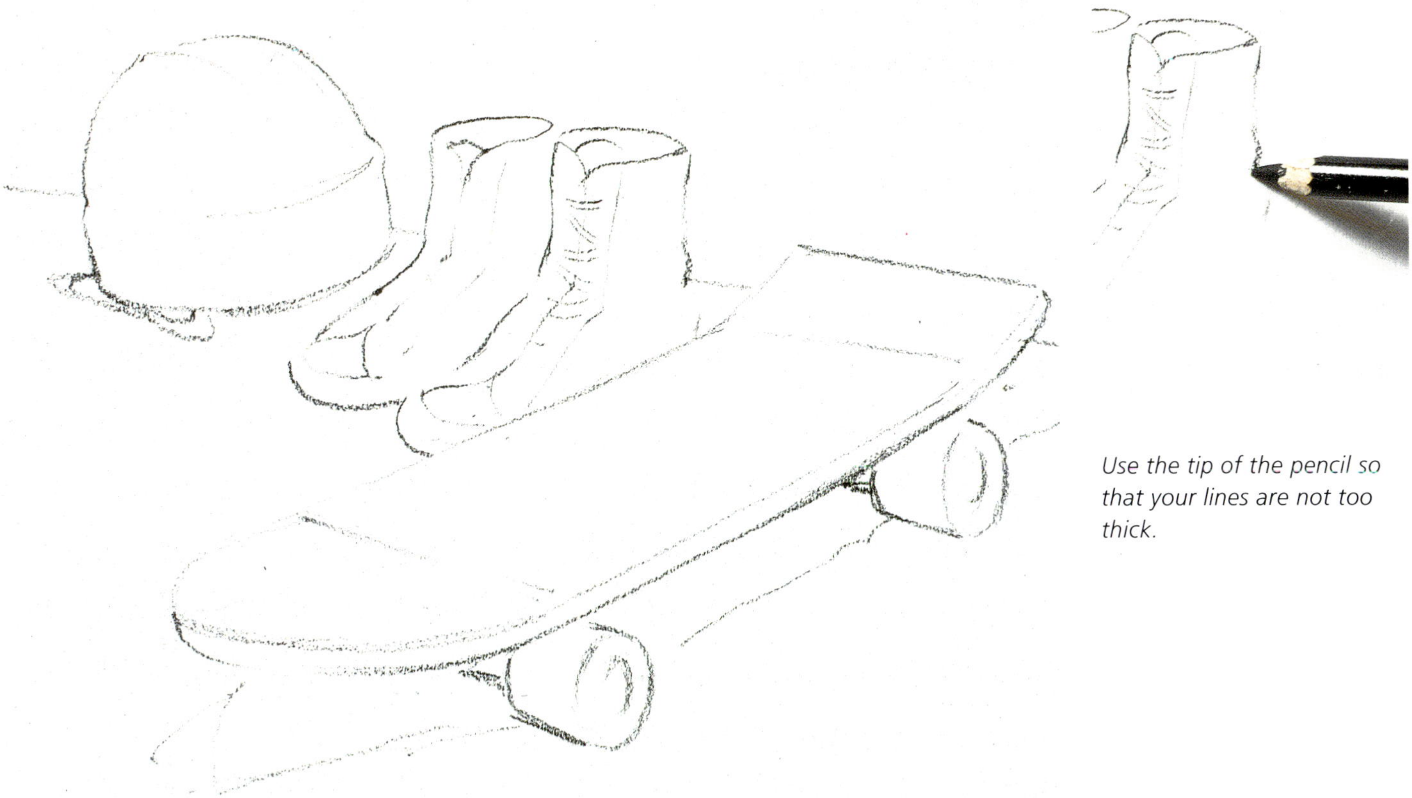

Use the tip of the pencil so that your lines are not too thick.

Once you have finished your initial sketch, go over the lines with a charcoal pencil. Draw the lines in one go, holding the pencil firmly so that you don't have any breaks in the lines. Draw in the main lines, the details, and the shadows of the skateboard and helmet.

Advanced projects

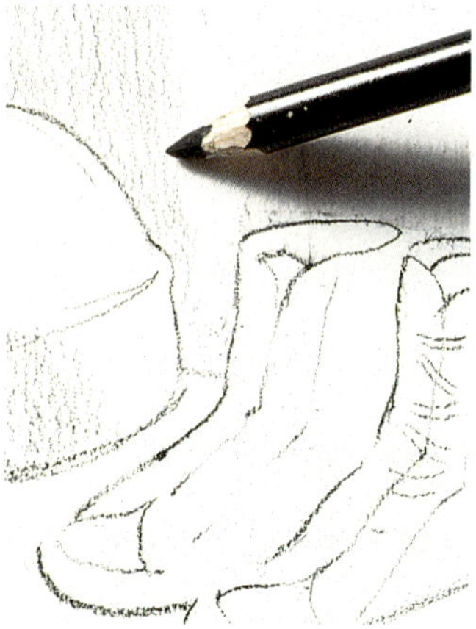

Hold the pencil tip flat against the paper and shade with parallel lines.

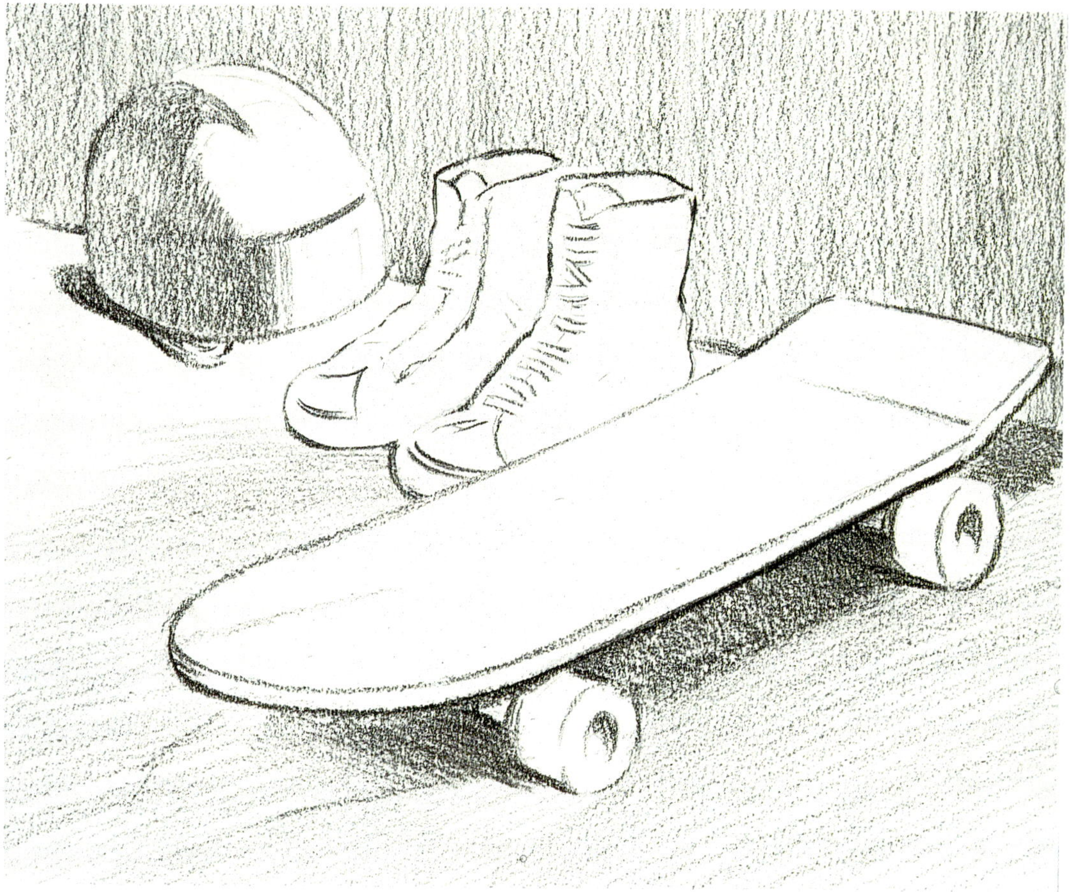

Draw vertical lines on the wall behind the helmet and boots. Use the flat edge of the pencil tip to do this, and keep the pressure even. Draw diagonal lines on the ground, pressing lightly. Start in the bottom right-hand corner and press more lightly as you move across. Then shade the darkest shadows on the helmet and under the skateboard.

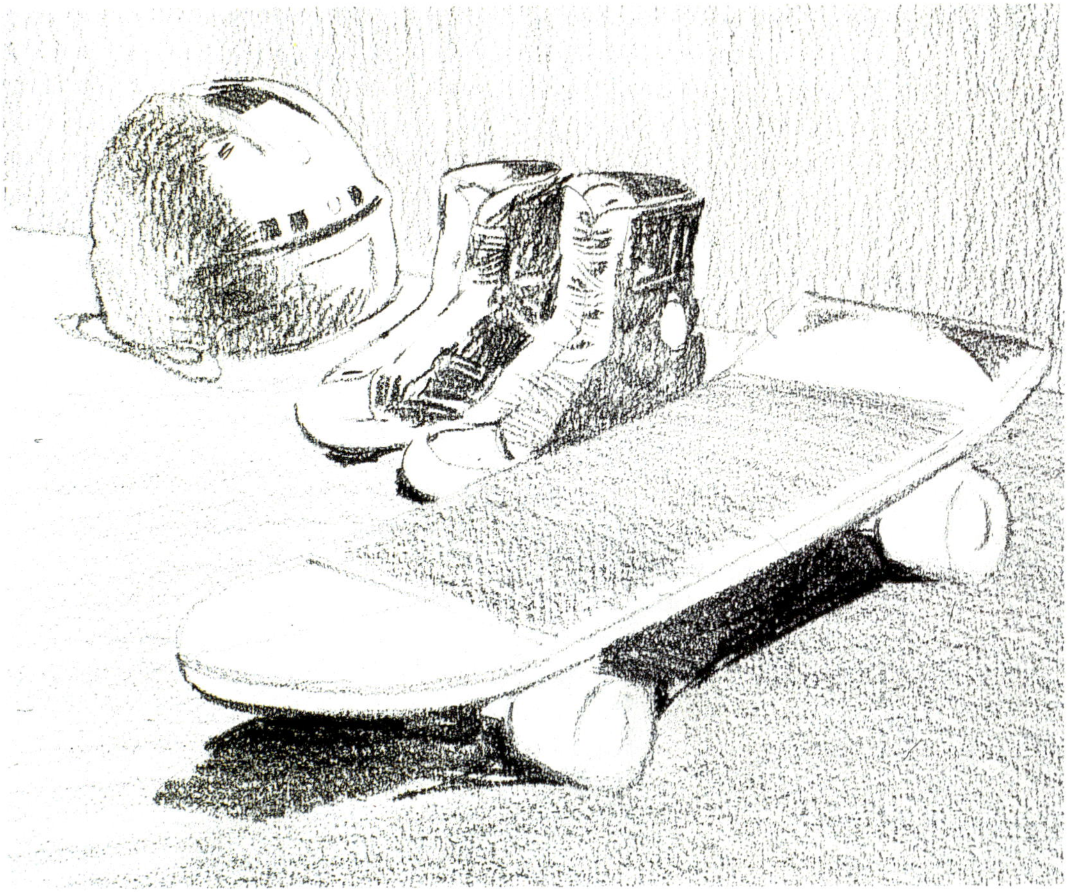

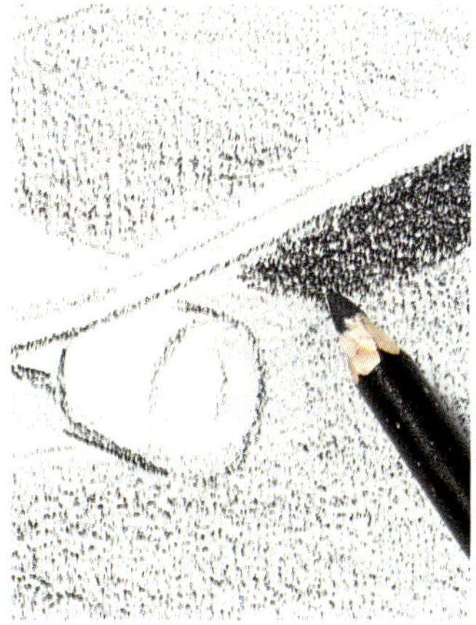

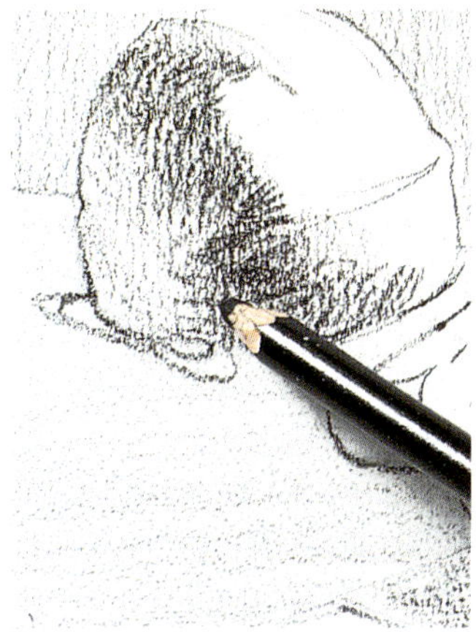

Strengthen the shadows. Shade in the upper part of the skateboard and shade an even tone on each of the boots.

Now draw lines in the opposite direction in the areas you have already shaded: the helmet, the boots and in the bottom right-hand corner of the picture.

Strengthen the shadow of the skateboard, going over it again and again.

Advanced projects

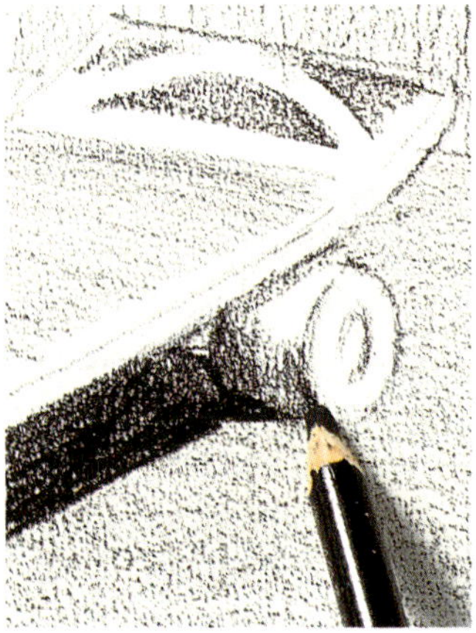

Shade the wheels of the skateboard with vertical parallel lines, and then go over the lower part of each wheel.

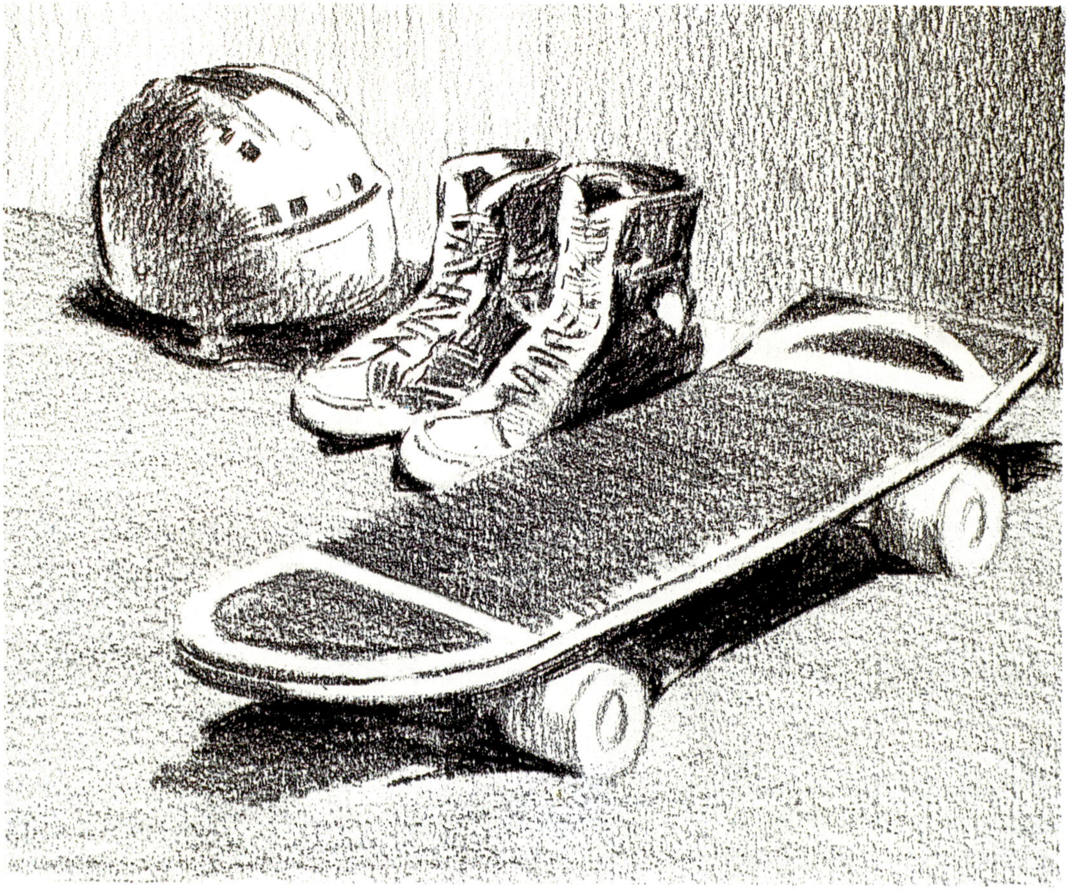

Darken some of the tones in preparation for gradating them later on.

Charcoal spreads very easily, so you do not need to draw many lines.

Gradate the top right-hand section and strengthen the shaded area in the background.

Draw in the sides of the skateboard.

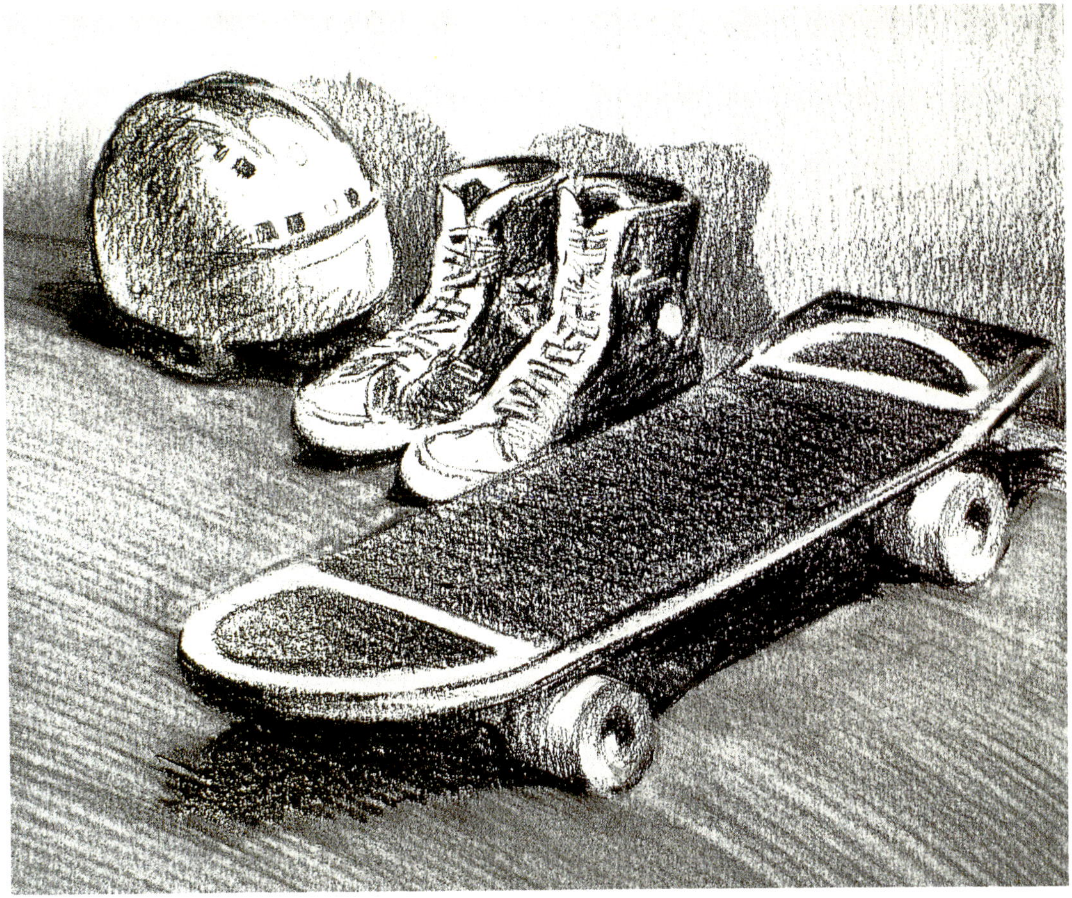

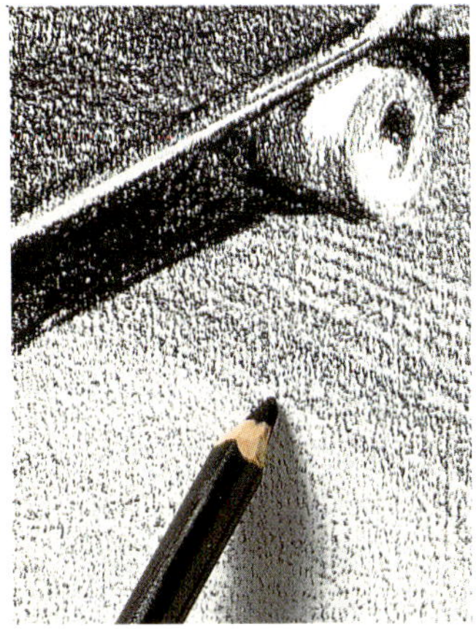

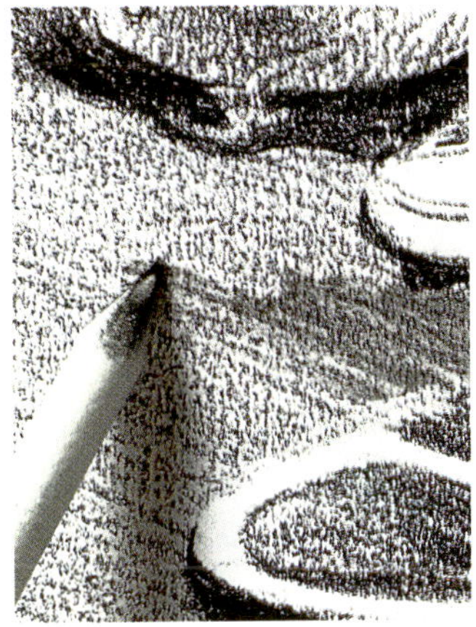

Now smooth out the shading in the top right-hand corner of the picture with your fingertips until you have an even grey tone. Use a paper stump for the shadows of the boots and the helmet. Then outline these shadows with new lines. Finally, shade with lines in the opposite direction next to the skateboard and even them out with the paper stump.

Advanced projects

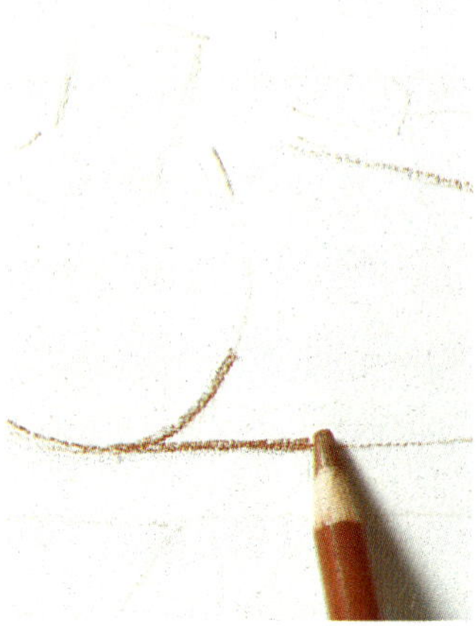

Block in the engine with simple geometric shapes.

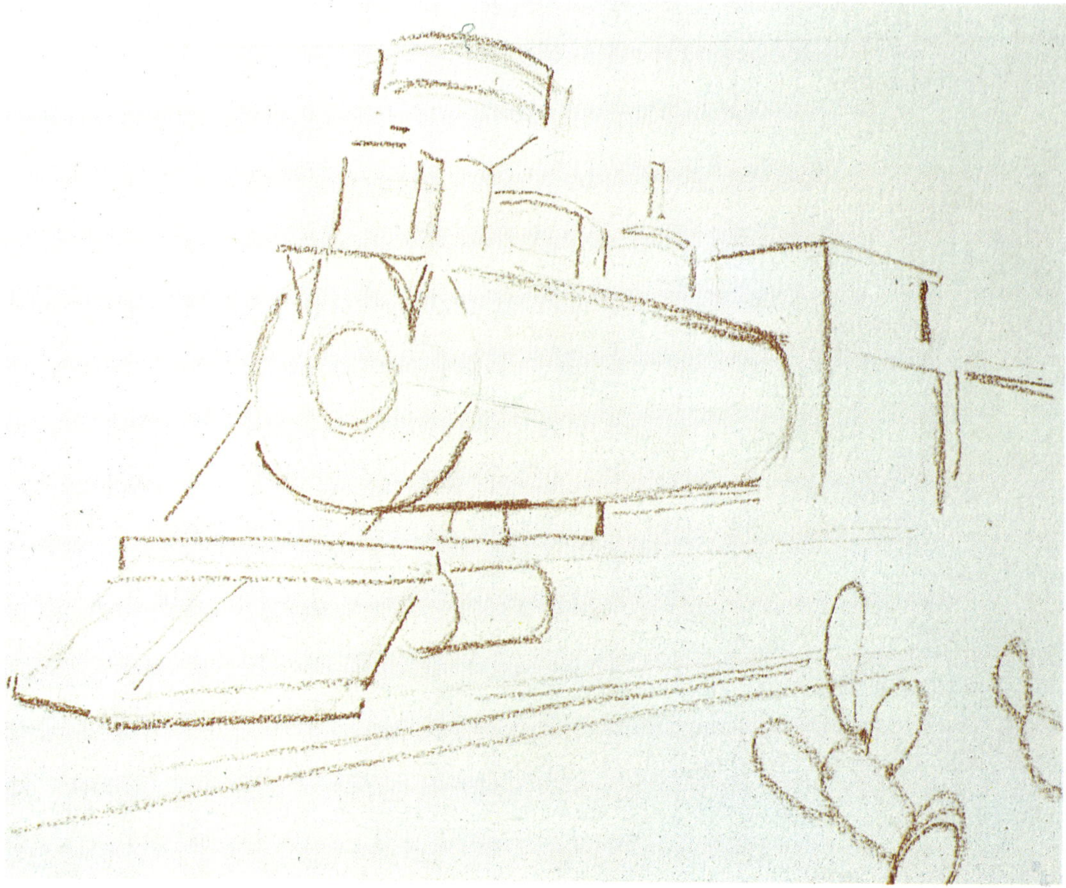

In this drawing you can use colour - in this case, a conté crayon.

Conté crayons are often used together with coloured pencils and pastels. This drawing will help you learn how to use a conté crayon.

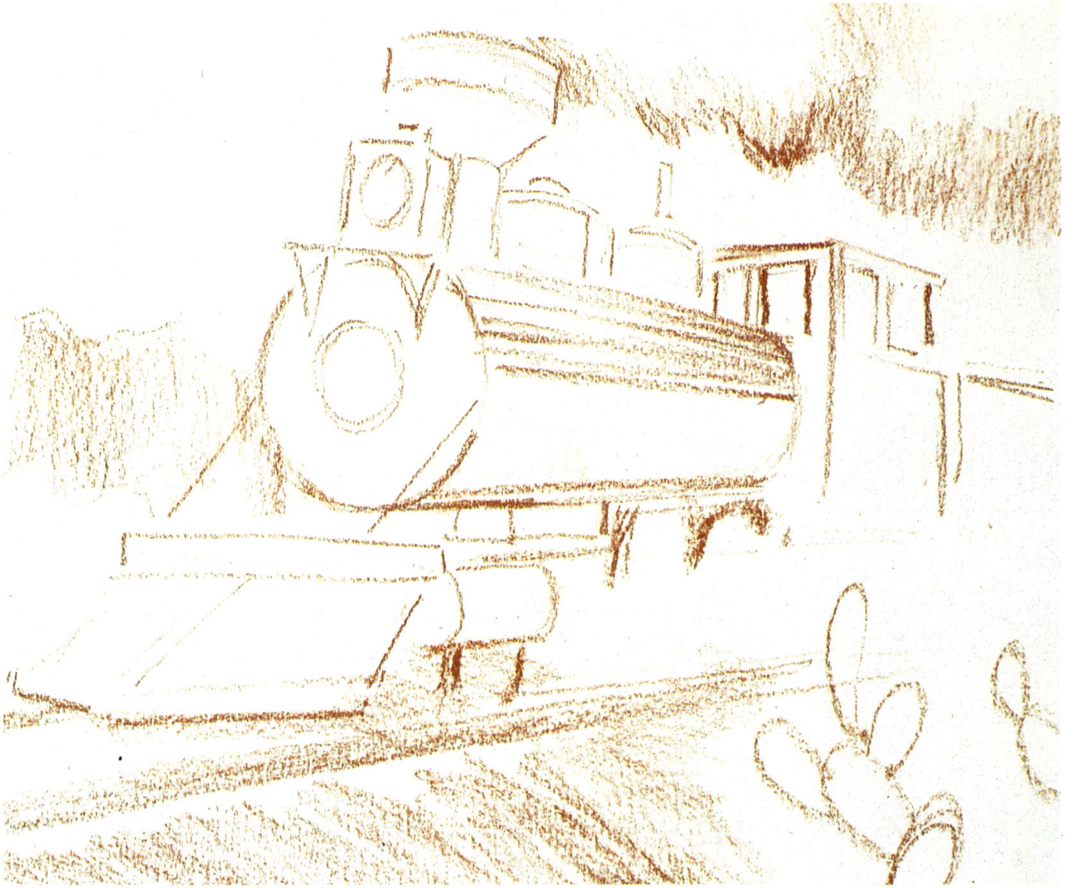

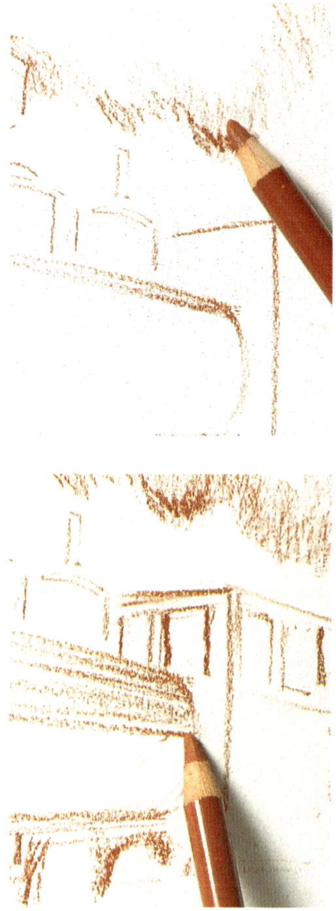

Hold the crayon in the same way as a lead or charcoal pencil. First colour the main background, the steam and the rails in the foreground.

Then put in some parallel lines on the boiler. Next strengthen all the sketch lines and begin adding details to the picture.

Advanced projects

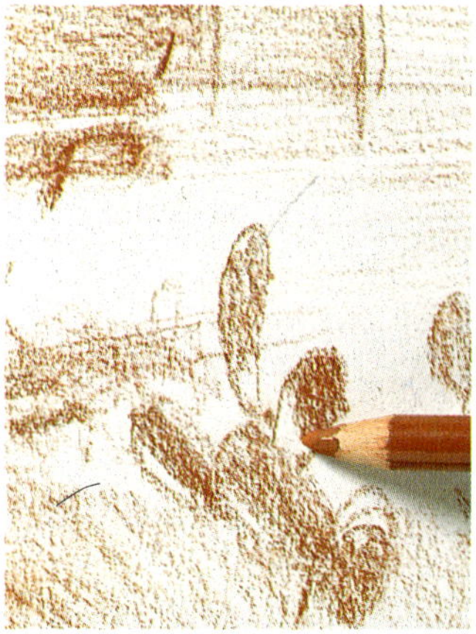

Colour in the cactus, but do not go over the lines of the drawing.

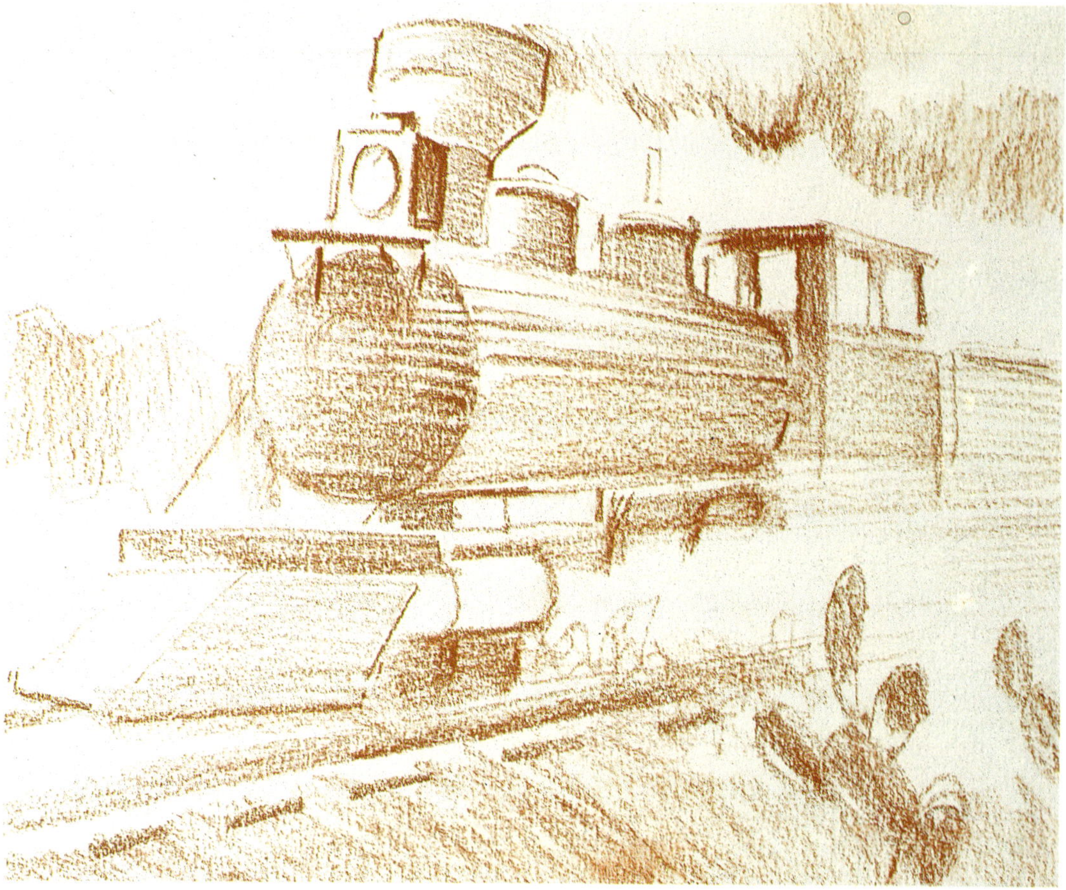

Now go on to work on the engine. Gradate the lower half of the boiler and draw parallel lines on the front. Shade the tender and truck in the same way.

Now draw in the darker lines of the lamp and chimney, and the curve of the boiler, holding the conté crayon so that you draw the thinnest lines possible.

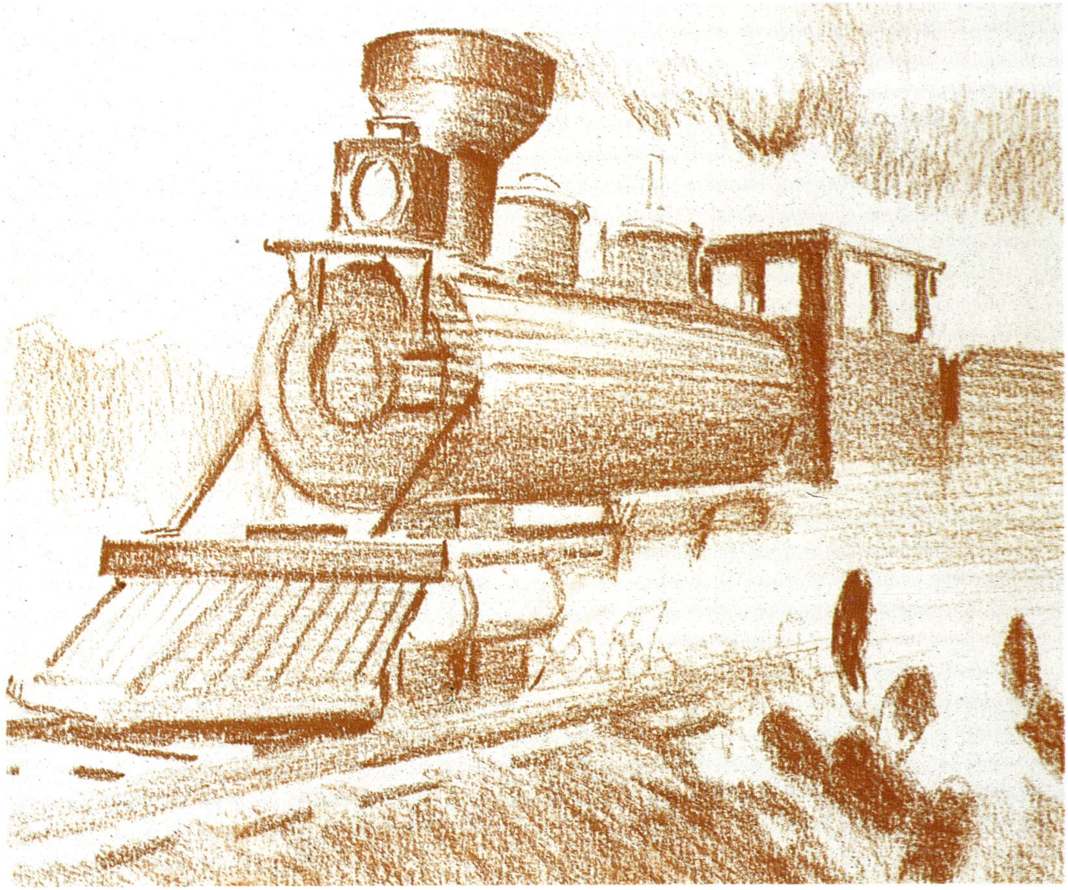

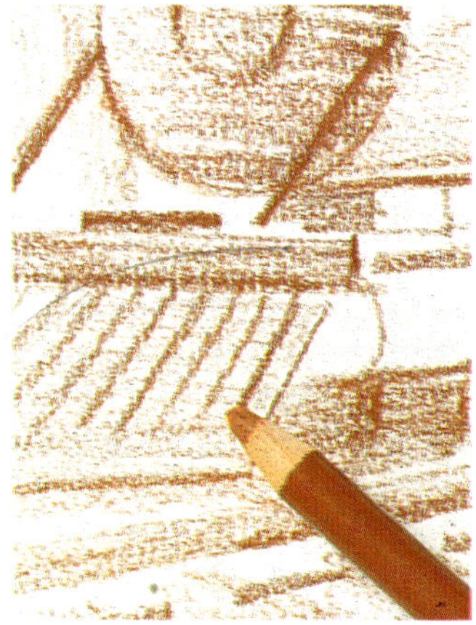

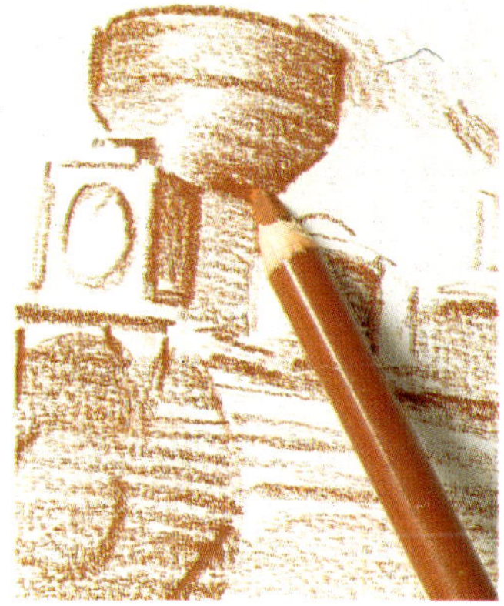

Darken some of the tones to create contrasts in the picture. Gradate the funnel and boiler by pressing harder on the conté crayon, then gradually reducing the pressure.

Draw parallel lines on the front of the engine and darken the tone between the track and the cactus.

Advanced projects

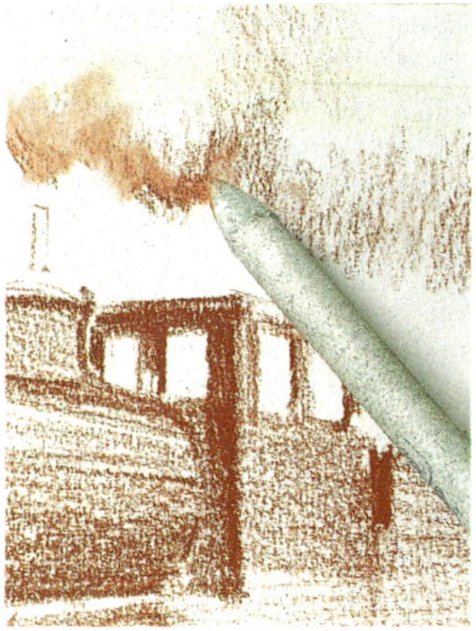

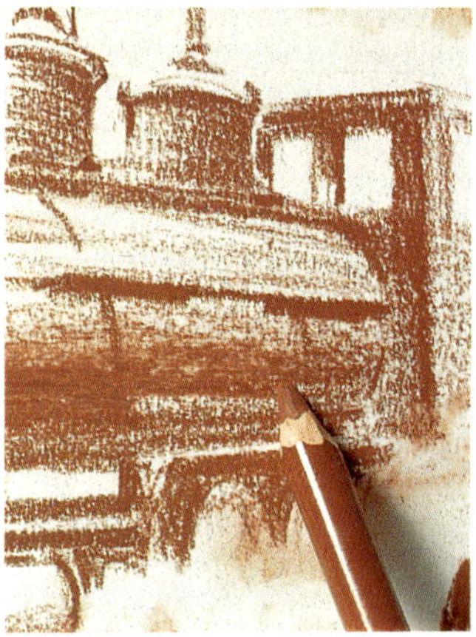

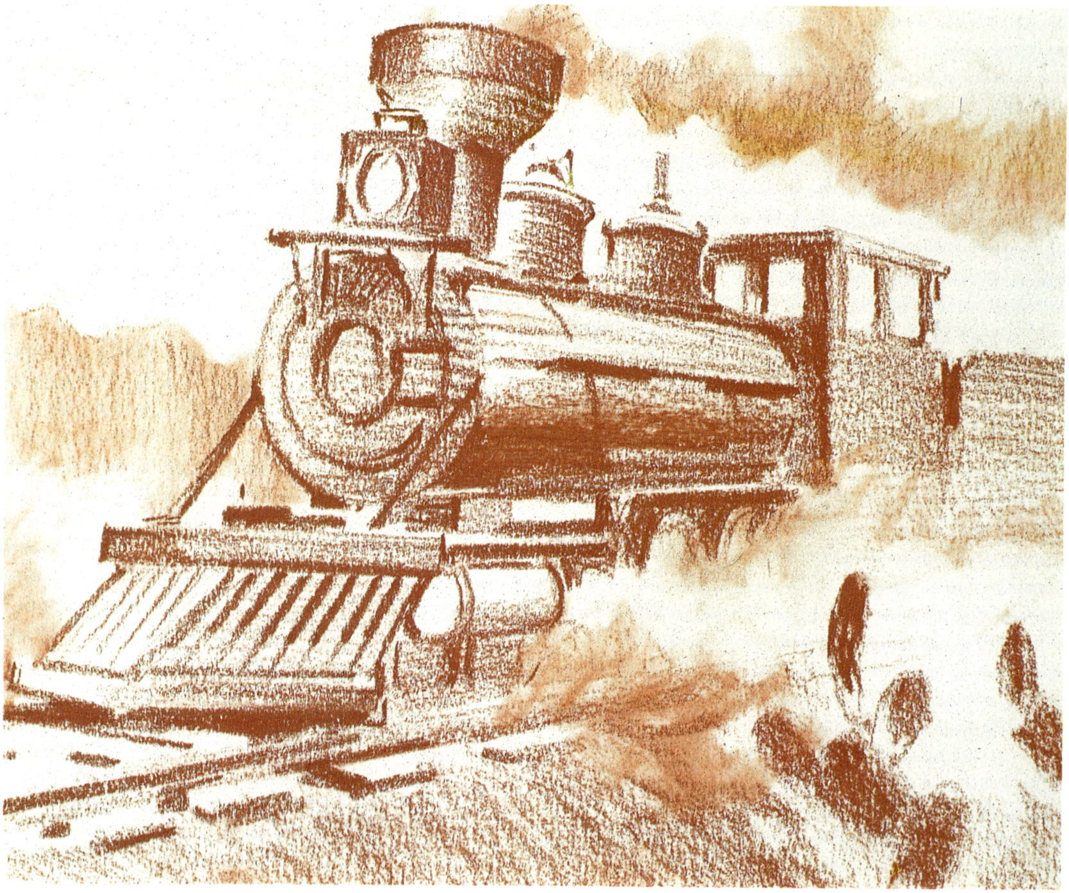

Even out the tones in the same way as you would with a charcoal pencil. Using a paper stump, rub gently until you have softened and evened out the crayon lines. Darken the tones of the lower half of the boiler, then outline it. Use the point of the crayon for outlining.

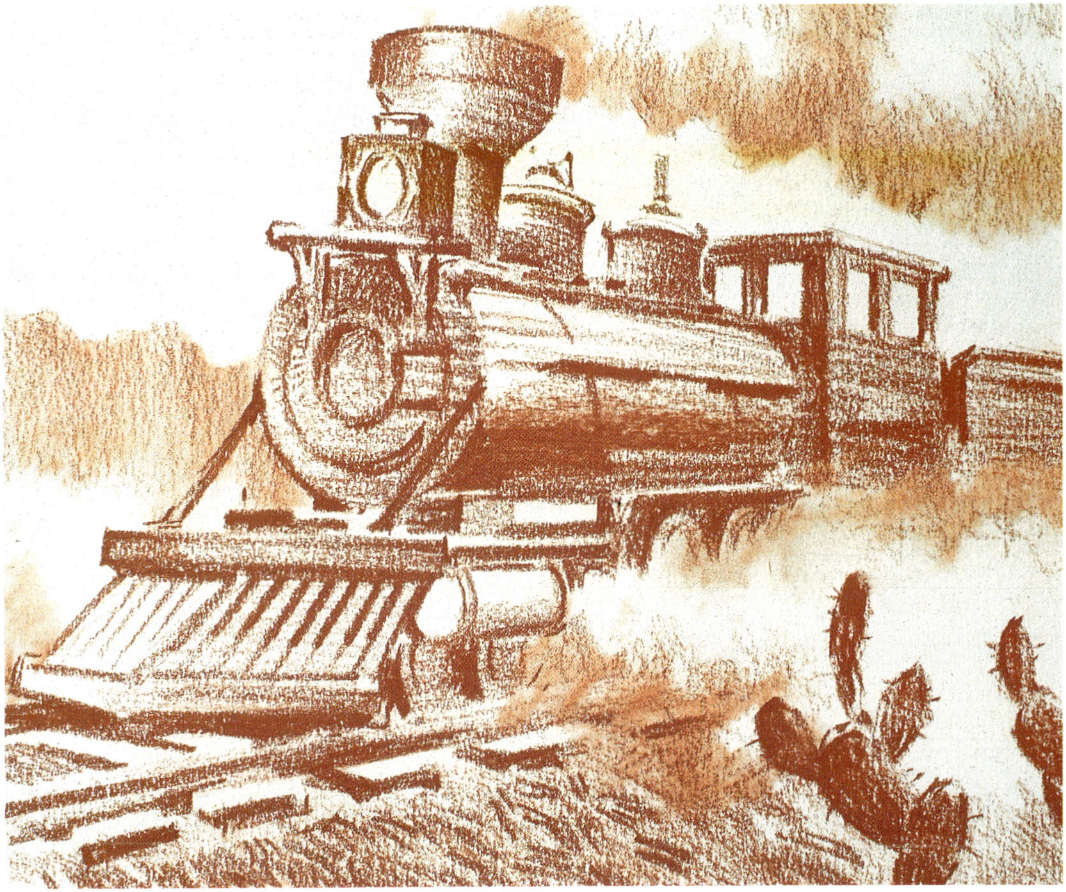

By shading with the conté crayon you can create an effect of billowing smoke.

Now it is time to add the final touches to the engine.

Go over the shadows several times with the conté crayon to create maximum contrast.

Draw some lines going in the opposite direction in the foreground next to the track.

Finally, draw some spines on the cactus.

Glossary

Block in. The first lines of a drawing, which sketch in the outlines and position of the subject, are blocked in. Blocking in is usually done with geometric shapes.

Clay. A mineral substance formed when rocks are broken down by water. Clay is used with graphite to make the lead in a graphite pencil.

Dimensions. The main measurements of the subjects you draw.

Fixative. A liquid which is used to fix charcoal drawings so that they do not smudge. The are many types available in art supply shops.

Gradation. Creating a series of greys from darker to lighter, or vice versa. It is used to show different strengths of shadows.

Graphite. A mineral substance used with graphite in the lead of a pencil. Pencils are softer or harder according to how much graphite is in them.

Proportions. The relationship in sizes between different objects in a picture. This is an important factor when doing your first sketches.

Putty rubber. A rubber which is used to rub out pencil strokes in solid areas. It can be moulded into different shapes.

Tone. Colour intensity or strength, which ranges from the darkest to the lightest.

Index

Foreword

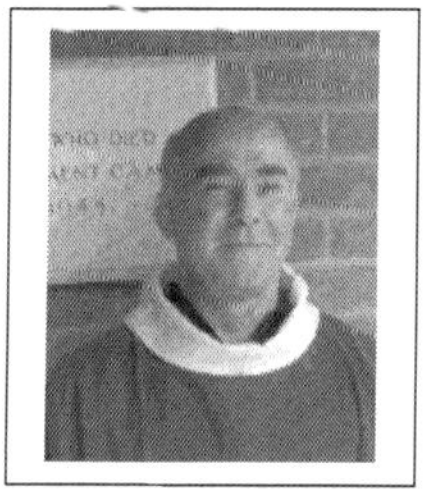

I am pleased to write this Foreword for this important booklet which has been produced so lovingly and conscientiously by Peter Wiseman, a member of the parish of Our Lady & St Thomas of Canterbury here in Wymondham.

In this Jubilee Year when we celebrate 60 years of service to our nation from Her Majesty Queen Elizabeth II, the Olympic Games and the Paralympic Games, we enthusiastically add our Catholic voices to the millions throughout the country and ask you to join with us as we celebrate one hundred years of the return of Roman Catholicism to Wymondham. This year we also celebrate the Diamond Jubilee of the opening of our church and the Golden Jubilee of the formation of our parish. 'We give thanks to God and bless his name' (Psalm 100) as we celebrate 100 years of service, commitment and witness.

I hope you will enjoy reading this most interesting booklet.

Father Dick White
Parish Priest
Our Lady & St Thomas of Canterbury
Catholic Church.
Wymondham

Acknowledgements

The author gratefully acknowledges the help of the East Anglian Diocesan Archive, and Wymondham Town Council Archive. I would also like to thank those who generously provided information, photographs and personal memories, not all of which could make it to publication due to space and time constraints.

Joan Bunn; Anne Dogget; Carol Donnelly; Mary Fairman; Paul Hawkins; Ann Hoare; John & Irene Lang; Ian & Jonathan Lester; Jenny Lysons; Jim Maxwell; Bernadette McIntosh; Mike Robinson; Tony and Helen Rossi; Jane Beck Sansalone; Sarah Short; Janet Smith; Sarah Standley; Kate & John Wood; and Phillip Yaxley.

Special thanks to Gill Page, for her invaluable advice, editing and publishing skills.

Finally, to my wife Teresa without whose patience, research and tolerance, this book would have faltered.

Apostolic Districts

1107 -1850

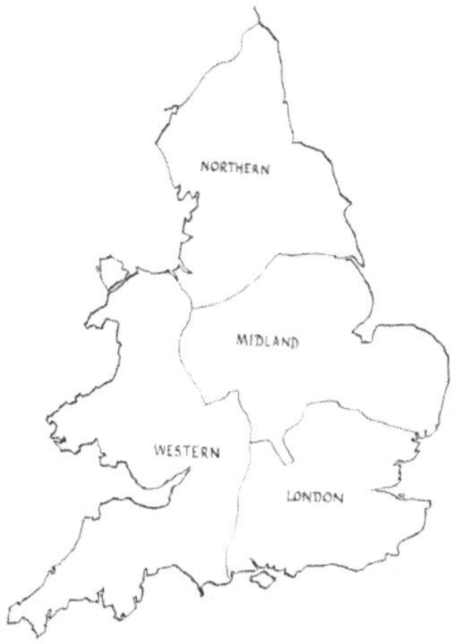

Apostolic Districts (pre 1850

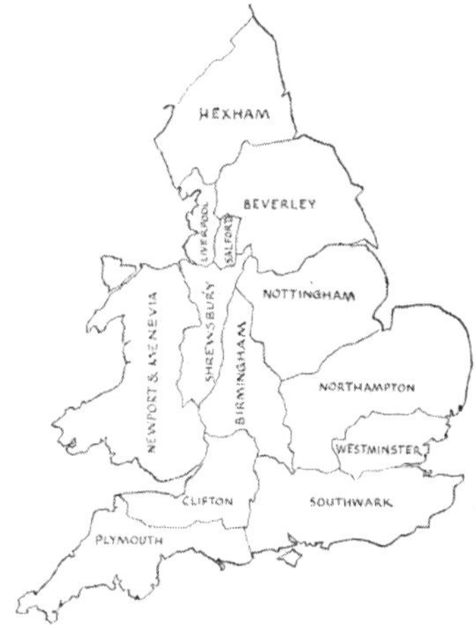

RC Dioceses 1850

Dissolution & Penal Times

The seed of Roman Catholicism in Wymondham was planted in medieval times as a cell of St Albans in 1107 during the Papacy of Pope Paul I. A monastery was built as a Priory for Benedictine monks on the site of the Saxon church by William D'Albini, Chief Butler to Henry I. Over the next 300 years it grew significantly in size, and its influence was such that both King Henry V and the Pope were petitioned in 1448 for it to be elevated to Abbey status and sever its link with St Albans. Once granted, less than a century later, the now independent monastery was forced to acquiesce to King Henry VIII's Act of Supremacy, turning it into a Protestant enclave. After 400 years of Papal jurisdiction, in the Papacy of Paul III, Roman Catholicism in Great Britain was banned by statute, its Districts abolished, and practice of the Faith driven underground.

Locally, the practical savagery of dissolution was put in the hasty hand of the King's agent, John Flowerdew of Hethersett, Sergeant at Law, who not only decimated this symbol of Papal authority, leaving the Abbey buildings largely destroyed and bereft of once sumptuous glory, but also sowed the corrosive seed of mistrust between state, church and citizen, that was finally vented in 1549 at Kett's Rebellion. Wymondham was truly a microcosm of wider religious, political and social turbulence which showed no signs of abating even after the deaths of Henry VIII and succeeding monarchs until the nineteenth century.

Penal Times were extremely grim, and Mary Tudor's (1553–1558) attempt at restoring Catholicism as a National Faith was short-lived and bloody. Within a year of Queen Elizabeth I accession she had revoked Mary's changes, reinstituted the Parliamentary Act of Supremacy and enacted the Act of

Uniformity in 1559 thus causing the practice of Roman Catholicism to become concealed again. Over the next two centuries The Faith declined critically. It was only prevented from dying out by the sustained efforts of tenacious souls who clandestinely persevered to bring the Holy Mass and the Sacraments to loyal Catholics. Nationally, Catholic numbers declined from half the nation in 1559 (population 4 million) to less than one tenth of it (60,000 of 7½ million population) by 1780. Even so, The Faith somehow survived and was maintained.

Diocese of Northampton

1850 - 1976

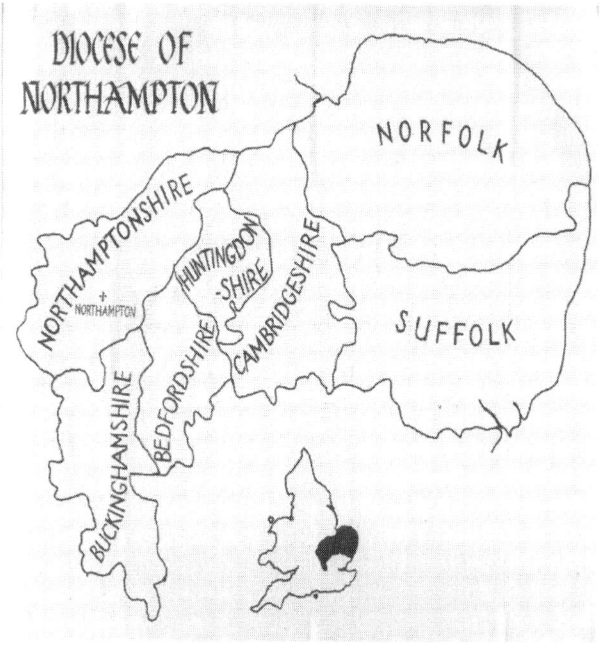

Diocese of Northampton 1850 - 1976

A Catholic Presence Reborn

Hopes of re-establishing the Faith waned until political expediency gave rise to the Catholic Relief Acts of the early 1790s. In practice, amongst other things, this granted the legal right to build chapels again and allowed overt Roman Catholic worship; as well as enabling Catholics to re-enter certain areas of professional life. These concessions and subsequent Acts saw Catholic numbers grow quickly. The Catholic Emancipation Act of April 1829 finally heralded a reintegrated Faith although it took three years to come into force. At this time Pope Pius IX re-established church governance by the creation of Provinces, Arch-Dioceses and Dioceses throughout Great Britain. However, for rural Wymondham still exhibiting tangible evidence of its heritage, Catholicism did not resurface here until the last decade of the 19th Century, and then for just 10 years. From gestation to rebirth took another decade before Bishop Keating, 4th Bishop of Northampton resurrected the Faith anew in Wymondham through one of its evangelising Motor Missions over East Anglia. This fledgling community was part of the large Northampton Diocese and guided by an Auxiliary Bishop until 1976 when Pope Paul VI decreed in *QUOD ECUMENICUM* that East Anglia be created as a Diocese for the Counties of Norfolk, Suffolk and Cambridgeshire. When in 1998 Peterborough became a unitary authority, it was added to the new Diocese, although as part of Cambridgeshire, it was already within the Diocesan boundary.

A Home for a Poor Mission: Cock Street

During World War Two Wymondham's sense of Catholic heritage was rekindled. Its Poor Mission Church, established as a result of a Motor Mission's arrival on the King's Head Meadow on August 8th 1911, had cause for joy. In April 1940, a

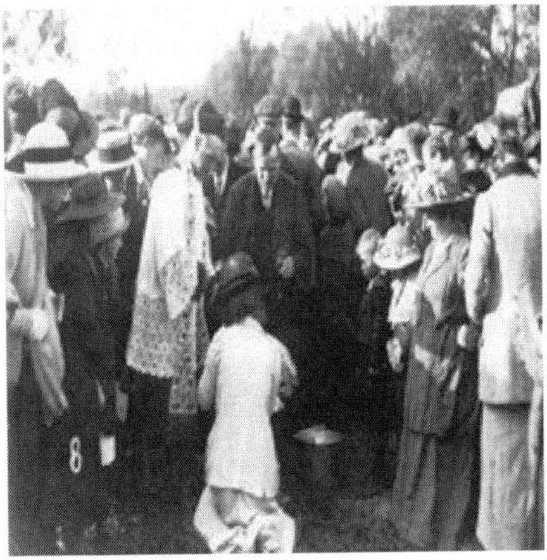

certificate, signed by Arthur Riddel, 3rd Bishop of Northampton, and dated *4th Decembris 1893*, was given to Fr. Ketterer by Mgr. Squirrel. It had been found in an old chest in St John the Baptist Church, Norwich (now the Roman Catholic Cathedral and See of the Bishop of East Anglia). This certificate has not survived, but Fr. Ketterer recorded in the Mission Book the details of the Faculty it granted: the Erection of Stations of the Cross in *'Ecclesia Sacratissimi Cordis DNJC apud Wymondham*'. (Church of The Sacred Heart of Our Lord Jesus Christ in Wymondham).

Little is known about this chapel which, ironically was in the shadow of its great antecedent, but it seems that it was a place of Catholic worship, initially served by Fr. Edmund Ford from Beccles until he left to become Prior of Downside. It was in the top bedroom of a private house – 22 Church Street. Originally built as Larner House in 1888, it was owned in 1893 by a solicitor, Mr Newton, of Messrs. Newton, Pollock and Wilson who had offices in Fairland Street – now the Leather Shop (2012). When he retired as County Court Judge in 1904 he moved to Watton and the chapel was given up. By 1912, it had become known as The Red House and in 1947 sold and re-opened as The Red House Guest House. It was finally absorbed as premises of the present Abbey Hotel in 1952.

The religious revival in Britain in the early part of the 20th Century did not exclude the Catholic fraternity. An evangelising 'Motor Mission', mentioned earlier, was sent throughout East Anglia and came to Wymondham and Dereham for two weeks in August during 1911 and 1912. This was a large car fitted out as a chapel and came with excellent preachers including Fr. Herbert Vaughan of the Redemptorist Fathers and three 'real ladies' that talked to everyone at the meetings in the town. Initially it set up in the yard of `The King's Head' public house (then opposite the Market Cross and a prominent coaching inn). A Mass took place on the Kings Head Meadow and attracted a huge crowd of interested onlookers and participants. An older resident of Wymondham confirms a newspaper report that the Old Town Hall in Town Green was hired every night for a week of meetings with question and answer sessions – free food ensured a packed audience who mostly had no intention of being converted but came for 'entertainment'! Indeed, such was their success that temporary premises were sought for its return the following year. Perhaps with an eye to Catholic heritage, enquiries were made, in vain, to use Becket's Chapel despite its (then) ruinous state.

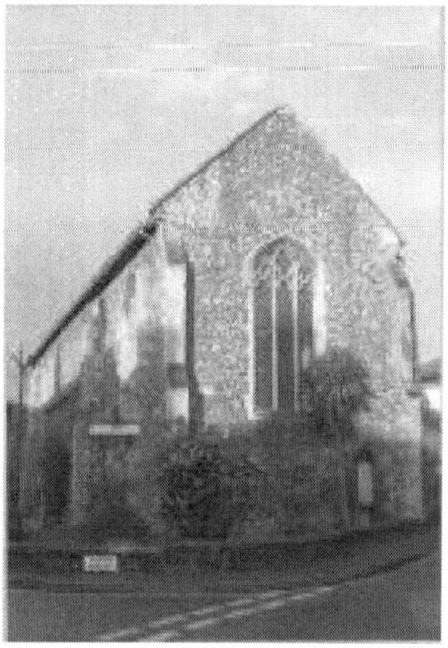

Chapel of St Thomas a Becket 1174

built by the son of William D'Albini

(Wymondham Arts Centre (2012)

However, a place was found by December of that year in Town Green. It was in the grounds of No.18/20 Cock Street and was owned by one Arthur Glasspoole, an organ builder. Formerly an organist at the Abbey (1867-80), he had built the workshop shaped like a chapel in about 1879 as an acoustically realistic place to sound organ pipes accurately. It was sited at the bottom of his garden, but could also be accessed from the lane beside his house.

Outside, its ecclesiastical shape looked every inch a place of religious worship: steep pitched roof, long pointed windows, a bell turret and weather-vane. Its eclectic style continued inside with a Holy Water stoup inset by the door, stone piscine and angel heads on the surround of the fireplace! It was rented to the Roman Catholic community and the timing of its discovery in December and its lowly workaday status must surely have resonated with them.

Here then, in the midst of a now very traditional and well established Church of England parish, was the first permanent centre for Roman Catholic worship in Wymondham since the Reformation. When the Motor Mission returned in August 1912 Holy Mass no longer needed to be celebrated in the open air as it had its own humble sanctified space. The success of the 1911 Mission was repeated and a week after the Mission had finished a Mission Priest was moved to pen an informal note to the Bishop with his impressions; '... *We concluded the eleven lectures on Sunday at Wymondham ... attendances ranged from 50 - 150.*

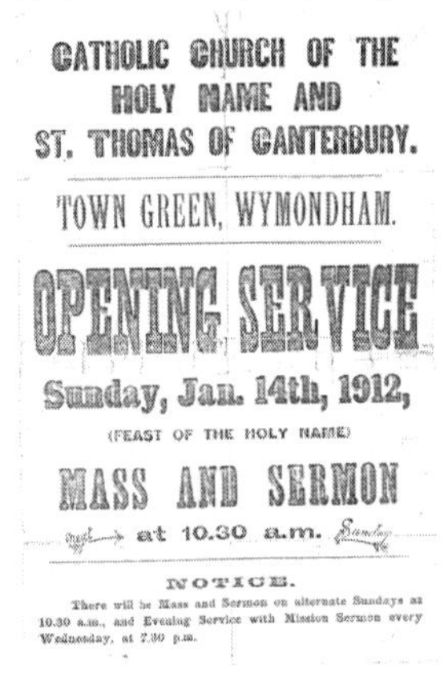
CATHOLIC CHURCH OF THE HOLY NAME AND ST. THOMAS OF CANTERBURY.

TOWN GREEN, WYMONDHAM.

OPENING SERVICE

Sunday, Jan. 14th, 1912,

(FEAST OF THE HOLY NAME)

MASS AND SERMON

at 10.30 a.m.

NOTICE.

There will be Mass and Sermon on alternate Sundays at 10.30 a.m., and Evening Service with Mission Sermon every Wednesday, at 7.30 p.m.

Poster of 1st Mission service

The building, which survives to this day, had its opening Mass on the 14th January 1912, the 2nd Sunday after Epiphany, by Fr. Henry G. Hughes. The tiny building seated 40 and as the local newspaper reported, had an inaugural congregation of 16 adults and 24 children and Mr Glasspoole played the organ for them. Prominent amongst them were Cecil and Laura Cross and Charles and Jessie Bird who had been at the Mission's open air Mass on the Kings Head Meadow the previous August. They had played a major part in locating and acquiring these temporary premises and they were amongst the first to make the difficult choice of conversion. Catechism instruction was initially given by a priest who came on his bike every fortnight, and also by nuns from The Little Sisters of the Assumption Convent, Norwich.

Cecil Cross converted first in 1912, after 6 months instruction, followed by his wife. Then on 26th June 1914 their youngest children, Adelaide and her elder brother Tommy became the first children to be baptised into The Faith in Wymondham for 400 years. At this Mass the honour of being Wymondham's 'Founder of the Faith' was bestowed on Tommy as he was 'done first'.

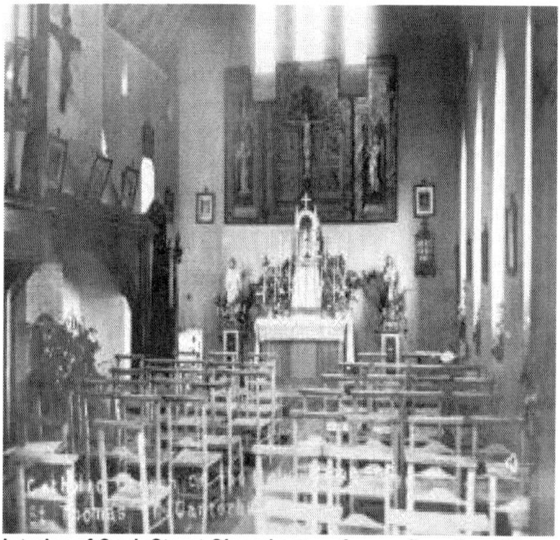

Interior of Cock Street Chapel set up for confirmation 26th June 1914

Conversion cannot have been an easy road for them and was not without personal cost. This local Catholic 'invasion' since 1911 had provoked bitter anti-Catholic feeling towards those who had switched religious allegiance. Cecil Cross was a wood-carver of some repute having had commissions from London and Bury St. Edmunds, but work became impossible to get as his business was boycotted. This was alluded to in The Missionary Gazette of September 1912 where it was reported that he had carved a Novena to The Blessed Virgin praying for business to improve. What more encouragement could a new convert need, than after 9 days of praying and working on it, the Anglican Vicar of Wicklewood gave him a commission for an Altar Frontal of carved oak which is still in situ in St Andrews & All Saints Church.

It was after their children's baptism that the combination of open hostility and dwindling business became potent reasons to move to Ipswich in early 1915 in search of work and more congenial surroundings for the family. Unfortunately, two years later, Tommy died there in a drowning accident. This tragedy caused the honour of 'Founder of the Faith' to be taken on by his sister Adelaide as the second child baptised in Wymondham. The responsibility of this honour was taken very seriously, as many older parishioners will testify. She died in 1995, having seen a permanent church built in her lifetime.

The Catholics' use of the Workshop Chapel lasted certainly until 1918 when the organ business of Arthur Glasspoole was sold. Whether they moved is not in doubt, but when, is not at all clear, but by 1926 the community had moved half a mile further down the road in Town Green, opposite the War Memorial.

A New Home: Town Green

Mass was still being said monthly but the search for better premises continued. Enquiries had been made in 1913/14 to use the Old Grammar School Rooms in Middleton Street, but as it had already been let for a three year period it was not available to them unless Northampton was willing to purchase it. Until an arrangement with The Colwyn School at 2a Town Green became possible, Mass was said somewhere but it is not known where. A Miss M.G. Randall had advertised her small private school for 'Girls and Little Boys' in the Abbey Church's magazine in June 1920 and it may have been as early as 1921/22 that the school was rented out to the Roman Catholic community as their second temporary home. The popular little school found space for them until under Miss Anna Smith's ownership, it transferred to her house at 8 Vicar Street until it closed in1937 due to lack of pupils.

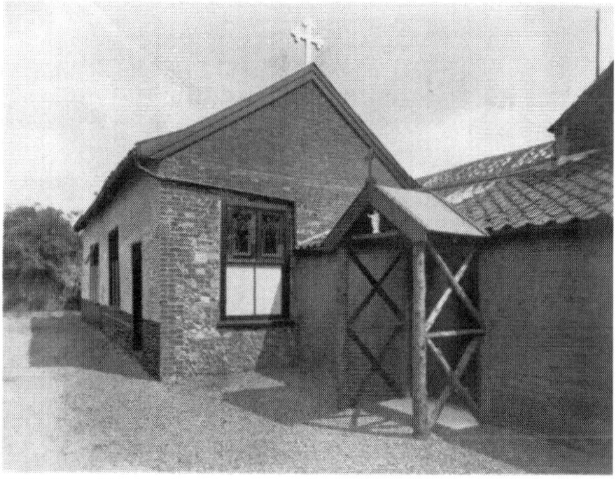

1926: Town Green
Our Lady & St. Thomas of Canterbury

A new Catholic resident also arrived in Wymondham in 1920. Capt. G.C. Gaynor MC, RAMC took up a position as one of the town's doctors. Recently discharged from the Army, he became an important figure amongst the community and prominent in its development over many years. It may well have been his quiet diplomacy amongst church authorities that encouraged them to find a priest for this small but resolute community. Several years later a priest was found. On his return from Rome via Port of Spain, Trinidad, Fr. Thomas K Phillips agreed to Bishop Cary-Elwes' request to become the Resident Priest in Charge at Wymondham's Poor Mission.

A Resident Priest

Coincidentally, ahead of Fr. Phillips arrival in Wymondham on 1st August 1926, the ostracised wood-carver and his family had returned in the February. As a test of Faith it was a triumph of fortitude that made them return to that same area, having been driven out just ten years previously. Sad to say it was only for a short time: Mrs Cross died in 1931 and Cecil Cross in 1936. In any event, since their return, obtaining work had improved for Mr Cross.

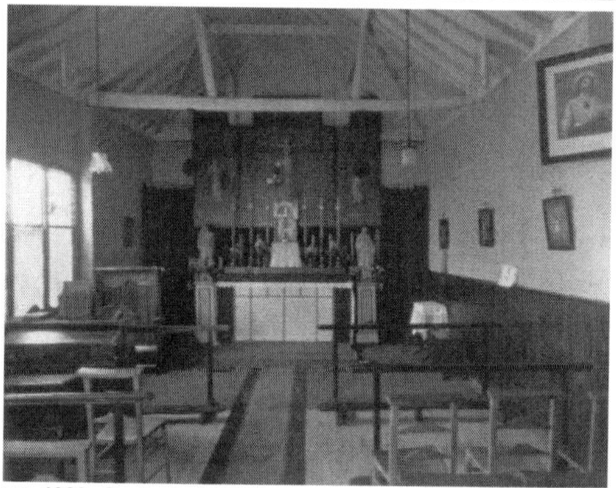

pre 1929: Our Lady & St Thomas of Canterbury, Town Green

Fr. Phillips hardly expected to be embraced on his arrival in Wymondham but this was the welcome he received on Mrs Laura Cross' doorstep. Her delight was palpable, and as far as the community were concerned, his arrival was an answer to fervent prayers.

The first page of the first Mission Book records:

'Rev. Thomas Kemp Phillips appointed Resident Priest by his Lordship the Bishop of Northampton'...

It also records that the Mission Church is now dedicated as Our Lady and St. Thomas of Canterbury.

The Parish of St. John's Norwich covered a considerable area and his mission was to serve the extensive rural district around Wymondham. For a few weeks he stayed at St John's Presbytery and bought a motor cycle for £50 to get around. He found his first lodgings, also temporary, at 1, Elm Terrace, Wymondham. This terrace had replaced one of four Maltings in 1904 and 'The Elms' next to it was formerly, owned by William Cann, the noted Wymondham Brewer. While there Fr. Phillips arranged to have use of their extensive grounds to say his daily office. Local lore has it that he buried a statuette of Our Lady somewhere in the orchard, although nothing has ever been found despite much of the ground being dug up for building works and various extensions when it became the site of the present church.

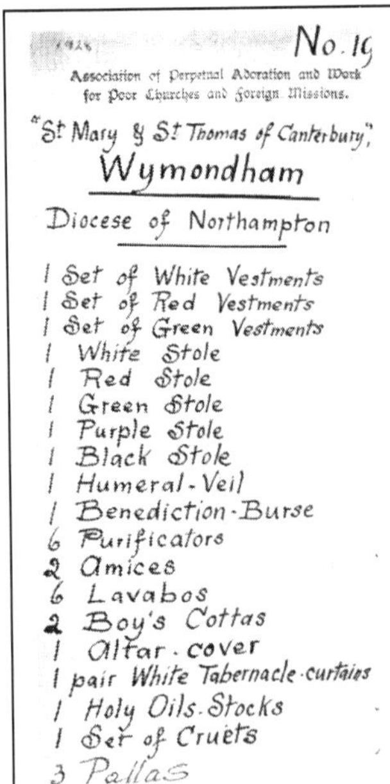
No. 19

Association of Perpetual Adoration and Work for Poor Churches and Foreign Missions.

"St Mary & St Thomas of Canterbury",
Wymondham

Diocese of Northampton

1 Set of White Vestments
1 Set of Red Vestments
1 Set of Green Vestments
1 White Stole
1 Red Stole
1 Green Stole
1 Purple Stole
1 Black Stole
1 Humeral-Veil
1 Benediction-Burse
6 Purificators
2 Amices
6 Lavabos
2 Boy's Cottas
1 Altar-cover
1 pair White Tabernacle-curtains
1 Holy Oils-Stocks
1 Set of Cruets
3 Pallas

Vestment List 1928

There was a lot of work to do and many practical things to set up before the Mission church was up and running. Finally, daily Mass was said from August 25th; with nightly Rosary and Simple Benediction in September. There was still the question of vestments for a Mission Priest. The National President of the Catholic Women's League wrote to the Bishop of Northampton on 26th October 1926 requesting permission to set up a Protection and Emigration work group in his diocese. Although this request seems not to have been followed up, the CWL became aware of a Mission priest who was in need of a set of vestments. Miss Gertrude Jarvis, Salford Section Secretary, wrote to him on 4th November mentioning that The Society of Perpetual Adoration and Work for the Poor Missions, an organisation run within the CWL, was able to supply the necessary vestments for Fr. T.K. Phillips, and included a list. Naturally the Bishop's response was immediate: *"reply Miss Jarvis & send a form to Fr. Phillips at Wymondham. Had better send him their letter when he returns today. Nov 12/26.'* By 17th November, Fr. Phillips had replied to the Bishop enclosing the completed application form to be forwarded to Manchester

By November 7th he had received permission to say Mass at Attleborough in The Griffin Hotel - another first Mass. It was perhaps not as fertile a ground as Wymondham, for although the Mass centre changed to The Drill Hall in March 1927 because it was longer and larger, by October 1929 he records simply that Sunday Mass is stopped! It was wartime, 1942, before his successor said Mass in Attleborough again.

Fr Phillips moved in January 1928, and again in May for a third time. This time it had more of an air of permanence: it was behind The Wool Shop in Town Green right next door to the Church. In that month, he also records that a Mr Grant came to live at the Presbytery, no indication of a particular role, but perhaps as a housekeeper? This much revered but sometimes caricatured role previously essential to Catholic parishes, but which no longer has a place today, has had its characters. For on January 3rd 1930, Mr Grant is recorded as leaving the presbytery, and Mrs Kenny arriving on the 20th as Housekeeper. While she might have fitted the latter category, parish folklore has it that she is principally remembered for dancing on the church roof on 'Old Year's Night' that year. How she got down or when she left has not been passed on!

Fr. Phillips was renowned for living a spartan existence and also recognised by the Bishop as being the most hard-working of priests. The neighbouring village and District of East Dereham which had been nurtured by Fr. Gray from Fakenham parish, was by 1930 in danger of losing their priest. After the struggle to get it established – he had been stoned on his arrival there some years earlier – clearly he didn't want to relinquish the fruits of his labours. When the Motor Mission arrived in 1911 it is reputed to have attracted 700 attendees. However, his time was being spread very thinly as he was also looking after the needs of Wells Next the Sea. Fr. Phillips pressed the Bishop for Dereham's temporary church, St Margaret Mary, to be included as part of his mission. After extended negotiation it was transferred to his care, holding his first Mass there on 23rd November 1930. Thus were many more miles added to his already extensive ministrations: an enormous workload.

Both communities were very much Poor Missions and during his tenure the church accounts show that they fully lived up to that description, often needing to be bailed out despite inventive means of income generation. In October 1927 Pew Rents were started – front seats 3 shillings per quarter, 2 shillings at the back! Church furniture was basic and adornment minimal in both places of worship.

All that the Wymondham church had to its name was a rudimentary Altar, framed pictures of the Stations of the Cross and single wooden chairs. In July 1928, the noted Arts and Crafts designer Mr McLean Leach of Cambridge, provided Fr. Phillips with a design for a beautiful oak Altar rail to be carved by Cecil Cross and Fr. Phillips immediately started a monthly collection to pay for it. This commission was completed and the rail in position in the church for Easter 1929, just two months before the benefactor's death. The final cost was £55 which included £25 for the carving. Several other carvings by Cecil Cross were completed for the church before his death in 1935 and have made the transition to the current church, although not all are on show, and some have succumbed to woodworm!

Fr. Phillips became very ill in July 1931 and he was subsequently in hospital for three months. Whilst he was ill, the Mission Churches spiritual needs were taken care of by the late Canon McBride, VG, who was then a curate at St John's. It was during this time that Dr. Gaynor kindly transported him from Wymondham to Dereham to say Mass. By 1934 Fr. Phillips had asked the Bishop for another Parish as he hadn't had a Sunday off in 8 years!

His legacy included two stable communities for the Mission church securing a sure foothold for Catholicism in the area and significantly increasing the extent of the Wymondham District. Not to mention negotiating a 10 year repayment plan to have electricity installed in the church and the presbytery at Wymondham in 1933. He is next located during 1938 at Thetford and Cambridge before transferring to Lowestoft in 1942. Anecdotally, the intervening time between 1934 and 1938 may have been spent having treatment and convalescing in St Joseph's Nursing Home in Beaconsfield. It is likely that he met Mother Leila of the Bon Secours (Good Help) Sisters there and established a connection that was renewed in 1945, when Fr. Phillips transferred to Sheringham with Miss Adelaide Cross as his housekeeper. In that same year, with Mother Leila, he oversaw the opening of larger premises for The Diocesan Residential Nursery of the Catholic Child Protection and Welfare Society which transferred its babies from Shefford in Bedfordshire to a large house behind St. Joseph's church on 20th June 1945. These 'Shefford' homes eventually fell victim to legislation (The Children's Act 1969) and through lack of funding closed between 1972 and 1974. By early 1947 Fr. Phillips was gravely ill. Miss Cross, who had dutifully tended him, and Mother Leila accompanied him to Granard House Nursing Home in Chelsea where he died on June 6th. His Requiem Mass was attended by Canon McBride and he is buried in Sheringham.

The desire for a permanent site was ever present and this might have come to fruition in 1935 if Fr. Phillips had been well enough to keep in closer touch with the diocese and gain their support. He had placed an option on some land and meadow barely 100 yards from their church building in Town Green, a prime location closer to the center of town, but the Post Office was in competition for it. This option would default without action, but until Fr. Ketterer was asked to take it over as Fr. Phillips successor it was unknown to the diocese. On the assumption that they were aware of it, he sent an urgent telegram to the Bishop about it; but it hadn't been authorised and the bid failed. The Post office was opened in 1940, but only the sorting office now remains in use (2012).

Another New Home: Norwich Road

Fr. John Joseph Ketterer succeeded Fr. Phillips, taking over the Chapel in Town Green on 15th October 1934. If Fr. Philllips' workload was huge, then Fr. Ketterer's was to prove even more extensive. Not only did he oversee another move of church premises, this time to a permanent site, but also managed a succession of assistant priests sent to help traverse the district to say Mass during the war years. The lack of entries in the Mission Book between his arrival and 1937 is perhaps indicative of how busy things were for him.

They say that priests develop the notion of being prepared for the unexpected and although this fact is not recorded, the following event has passed into folklore. Having settled in this preparedness was tested one Sunday morning as he robed up in the Sacristy: the floor gave way under his foot! He had gone through the floorboards! It transpired that that part of the former Colwyn School building had been built over the sawyer's pit of a timber merchant's premises next door. The ever-present sense of need came to the fore once more. If ever there was a need for a permanent site, it was then.

A Mission Church in a Stable

A large house, The Elms, at the junction of Bridewell Street and Norwich Road, came back into the frame as a potential site for the new Church. Mrs Leah Clements, a widow, had previously given Fr., Phillips free access to the grounds of her orchard to say his priestly office. This amicable arrangement evolved into an enduring friendship, which on her death in 1937, translated into the sale of the property to the Northampton Diocese in the November. While it was not in the centre of town, as preferred in 1935, it was in a historically significant position, bordering as it does the Kings Head Meadow where the first Motor Mission had held its open air Mass in 1911.

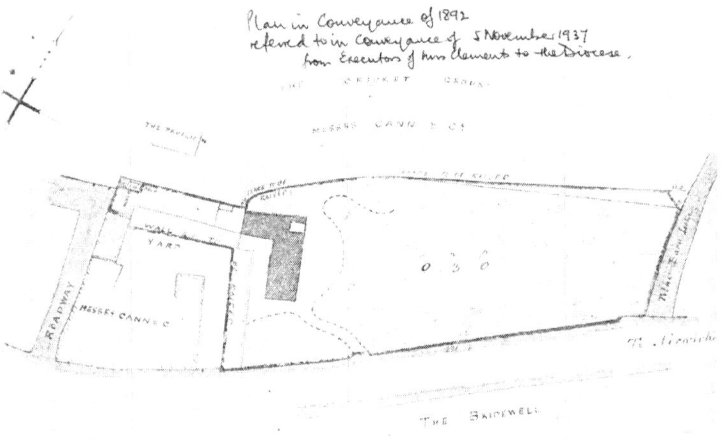

The New Church site

The sale was completed on the 5th November for £950. Wymondham's Mission Church at last had the permanence it had been seeking. Formerly a Maltings and Brewery Manager's house, 'The Elms' also had extensive outbuildings: a stable and coach-house attached to it. The joy and urgency of *'making a new House for Our Blessed Lord'* is indicated by Fr. Ketterer's entry in the Mission Book on Dec 26th:

> *"... I decided after considering the main part of the house as a possible church, to convert buildings comprising billiard room; coach house; wood shed and stable into a temporary church. The work was begun today and undertaken by: R Caddy, S Caddy, S Moore and John Thompson and others at times with the connivance of the writer. The work was done in the evening from 6-9pm by the light of paraffin lamps and was finished in 10 weeks.*

With notice given to relinquish the Town Green Chapel and his lodgings, the stable was transformed into a church with seating for 45.

However, things had not gone entirely as planned for Fr. Ketterer records in the Mission Book that, *'I myself was almost an invalid that week from fibrositis and influenza brought on by working in damp and cold conditions ....'*
What is not mentioned is that the planned opening of the little community's latest home had to be put back a day as a result. So it was Wednesday 6th April 1938 when the Church of Our Lady and St Thomas of Canterbury was Blessed into the service of Our Lord, supported by five priests of the locality including Fr. Phillips from Cambridge. It is worth noting that even though it was a newly converted building on a permanent site, The Lord's House must be debt free to be consecrated. In common with its predecessors, The Stable Church was only able to be Blessed and Wymondham and District's Catholics latest temporary home would have to wait for this final honour. But what a prodigious effort of joyful penance; continuing through Lent to ecstatic completion in time for its first public Mass on April 10th 1938, Palm Sunday. Apart from donations and benefactors' gifts it was completed for a recorded cost of £10! The unusual gift of time was

reported by 'The Universe' correspondent: *'a stranger from Falmouth, a Mr Bradley, acted as Cross-bearer for the procession from the new presbytery to the church' having given up a week's holiday to help in the final preparations of the building.'*

A very grateful priest also recorded particular thanks to some parishioners: *'Mr Moore and his sons for transferring all the house and church furniture; to Mr C Bird for fitting and fixing of all the seating including all the oak carvings of Cecil Cross'*

For all that, Easter celebrations must have been especially joyful that year. Just six weeks later, by Whitsun (5th June), The Stable Church and its priest were so popular that its congregation had increased. Clearly there was little room for expansion. Undaunted, the priest and his helpers set to and rearranged the interior *'between Whitsun and the following Sunday: the Sanctuary wall was knocked down and the altar moved further back and the woodshed was turned into a Sacristy.'* With another 30 seats available its capacity was almost doubled to 75 in just one week at a cost of £5 for materials!

The War Years

Premonitions of war were already prompting contingency planning in early 1939. Barely had the community settled into their new church, when Fr. Ketterer was strategically appointed as Chaplain to the Royal Air Force Station at Watton, saying his first Mass there on 5th March 1939. He still had the church community at Dereham to minister to, and in recognition of the practicalities entailed serving an additional Mass centre 10 miles away, he was granted assistance by priests from Walsingham Friars Minor on each first Sunday of the month. This was timely, as the next entry in the Mission Book states '*September 3rd WAR*'! Noted beside it is *'Mass at Watton RAF Station every Sunday and supply every Sunday from Walsingham. There are rumours of more aerodromes......'*

He must have spent a considerable amount of time getting to places. As a Poor Mission a motor car could not be supported and Fr. Ketterer became well recognised as the Priest on a bicycle! Whilst the extra -parochial work caused by the influx of people to the area swelled his congregation at various times, ministering to the Irish labourers, brought over specifically for building airfields locally, entailed much more travelling. In addition, until their own chaplains arrived, he also said Mass for the advance parties of the USAAF bomber squadrons based nearby, especially Hethel.

In times of war, religion gives people something to focus on, enabling them to work through its traumas and privations. And so it was for the Catholic community of Wymondham District. Bishop Leo Parker's visitation to confer the Sacrament of Confirmation at East Dereham on the afternoon of March 15th 1942 was not going to be postponed. There must have been a substantial number of confirmandi as the Assembly Rooms were hired and 3 extra priests were present –

Fr. Brewer, Fr. Pitt and an Army Chaplain. It was evidently a major occasion as the Bishop also concelebrated Mass there in the morning to a very large congregation and *'preached on the great inheritance we had from pre-reformation days; and the living monuments in our Parish Churches....'*

Hethel is nearly 4 miles from Wymondham, and the aerodrome that was being built was to provide a permanent base for the American USAAF bomber squadrons. It was to be the home of the 389th Heavy Bombardment Group which had been assigned to the Eighth Air Force, and in England, formed part of the 2nd Combat Bomb Wing in Norfolk with the 445th Bomb Group at Tibenham and the 453rd at Old Buckenham. By early June 1942, it was almost completed and personnel were arriving throughout June and July. Their first squadrons soon became operational and remained so until their departure in May 1945. However, it was some time before they had their own Catholic Chaplain on base, and Fr. Ketterer included the Americans in his pastoral care with the Irish labourers. Fr. Gerald Beck, OFM, a Franciscan Friar, nicknamed 'White Flak' because of his white hair and sharp tongue when telling airmen off for bad behaviour, was a dynamic and generous man popular with the airmen. Fr. Beck was most appreciative of Fr. Ketterer's pastoral efforts in advance of his arrival in late August 1943. They struck up a close bond and he was a great support to him thereafter. Indeed, he even arranged for the ladies of Wymondham Parish to make vestments for Fr. Beck as well as all the altar

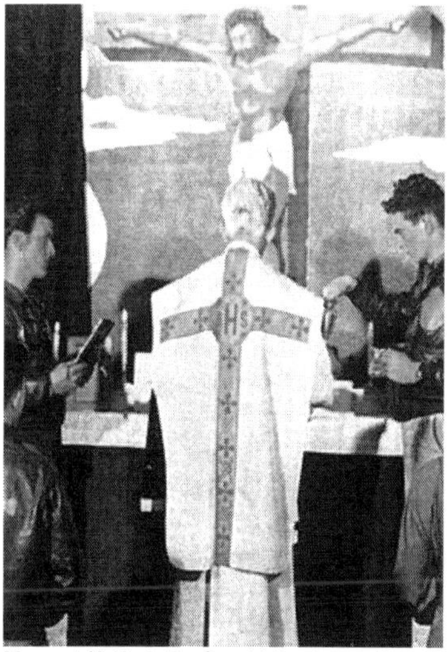

Mass at Hethel: Fr. Gerald Beck wearing the

linens for their chapel with the mural of the Crucified Christ behind the altar painted by his lay assistant Bud Doyle.

It was Fr. Beck's style to mingle with his 'flock', and he and other chaplains on base would attend crew briefings before combat missions and then sit in a jeep on the edge of the runway making the Sign of the Cross over each plane at take-off. Whether Fr. Ketterer ever joined them is not known; but this great priestly alliance endured until the end of the war. His support was reciprocated often in kind; sharing many a meal with them and in the form of monetary support on several occasions. The Americans were very aware of their affluence and the disparity between their facilities and Wymondham's impoverished Mission church. On one of many occasions, when he returned from a raid over North Africa Fr. Beck demonstrated his generous nature at Mass when:

> *'... he asked for a 'silent collection'. A silent collection had to be a ten shilling note or a pound note. The ten shilling was equal to $2.00 and the pound, $4.00. The collection came to $1200. This huge amount astonished the poor, struggling English priest. He felt deeply grateful and continued to come on his bicycle to help out saying Masses, hearing confessions and novena services.'*

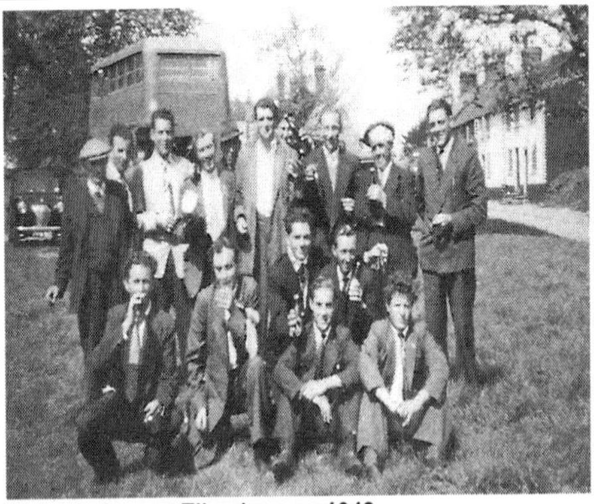

Irish Workers at Tibenham ca.1942

Fr. Ketterer's workload increased as Irish workers began arriving to build more aerodromes, over 850 during the next couple of years, at Snetterton, Shipdham, Tibenham, and Deopham, amongst others. Help finally arrived in November 20th when Rev. O. Baker arrived as his curate. On the plus side, the capital debt on the church at Wymondham was now down to £680.

For the next year or so it must have been frantic, as he only had time to record Fr. Bull's arrival on May 26th 1944, and then nothing until the day before Palm Sunday on March 24th 1945 when this little church was registered for marriages. The uncertainty of war prompted marriage early in a relationship, sometimes in haste; and now the end of the war was imminent there was added impetus to 'tie the knot'! The first marriage here was celebrated by Fr. Ketterer just 9 days later on 2nd April – Easter Monday – between Elizabeth Mary Boughen of Wymondham Parish and Staff Sgt. F O'Donnell USAAF. Several years ago, after a long and happy marriage, the now widowed Mrs O'Donnell wrote to the new church and visited it. In a subsequent letter she recalled that *'there was so little room between the chairs [of the stable church] that they [as husband and wife] had to walk down the aisle in single file!'* But a few days after this happy occasion for the church, it became tinged with sadness as Fr. Bull left on the 6th April and was detained in hospital. A cruel irony with the end of the war in sight!

It was perhaps more a thanksgiving than a celebration when on 8th May no mention is made in the Mission Book of [VE Day]; but his entry for May is characteristically brief, *'First week of leaving, in large numbers, of American personnel from this area. Shipdham and Hethel first affected....'*

May 14th saw movement orders for the 389th to be repatriated to America. For the last time, they invited their English friend, Fr. Ketterer, to share a farewell Sunday dinner. *'Once again they gave him a large sum of money they had collected for him. He was so excited he could not eat dinner this time.'* Within a month, between 20th May and 25th June, all the Americans had left the area. In any event, a hint of normality reappeared in parish life, and: on July 29th he *'placed fresh*

Stations of The Cross in the church which were presented by Sir Pierce Lacy, Bart.' And on August 15th [VJ Day] a *'Children's Pilgrimage to Walsingham was made. 60 children took part and 28 took Communion. He was assisted in the Mass at the Slipper Chapel in the morning and at Benediction in the afternoon by Major Case and Fr. Pacifus.'*

With the country resuming an air of nonchalance about daily life, Fr. Ketterer received a new set of Stations of The Cross from Fr. Coakley on September 8th, which he in turn took the following day to Sheringham to be erected in the Chapel of their New Children's Nursery, the residential home overseen by Fr. Phillips in June 1945 and run by the Bon Secours Sisters, with whom he had had much contact.

Fr. Ketterer was a well-liked man and priest, who spent his time making plans for a new church. But this challenge was to be a successor's test as he was sent to Kings Lynn in late 1946. His legacy is undeniable: a permanent site with priest's house fully paid for, and £2,500 towards the building of a new church, thanks to the generosity of USAAF personnel and Irish labourers. He moved just once more to Hunstanton in 1955, from where he retired in 1972. He died in 1973.

Development: Norwich Road

It was the day before Old Year's Night 1946 when the Poor Mission's next Priest In Charge arrived after a very different wartime experience. Fr. Cowin had been ministering to fellow Catholics as a prisoner of war.

He converted to Catholicism aged 21 and was an assistant priest at Newmarket before transferring to St. John's, Norwich, in 1939. He had spent little time there before WWII was declared, and he joined up as a non-combatant Chaplain attached to 196 Field Ambulance RAMC. It was his misfortune to be one of nine British Army RC Chaplains caught up in the surrender of Singapore in August 1942 with other East Anglian men of the 18th Division. Originally destined to defend it, they shared instead the brutal conditions of imprisonment in the Japanese POW camps for 3½ years. He emphasised his non-combatant status by always wearing his tropical priestly cassock rather than uniform. Whilst it gained him no privileges, it was a tangible symbol for fellow FEPOW to keep faith (and hope) alive. To keep focussed on the beauty of the future, he built an RC chapel in three different camps. Denial of spiritual succour is a tool of all oppressors, and this was evident, for despite making *'scores of applications to minister to Catholics in adjoining camps with no RC minister, the Camps Commandants' always refused him permission.'* (*Cross on the Sword p263*). The scarcity of bread and wine

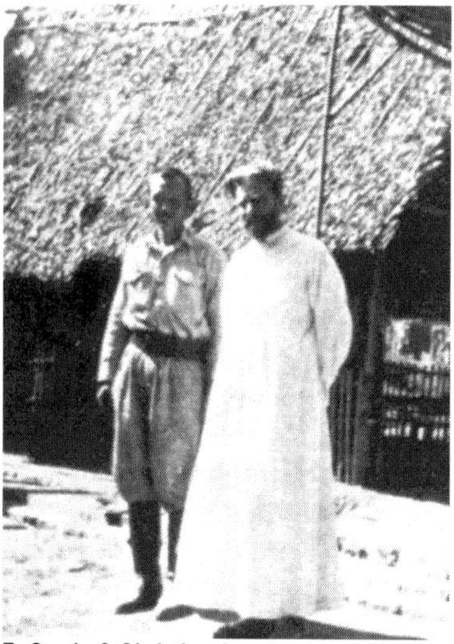

Fr Cowin & Christian Japanese Dr. outside the chapel built in Kanchanaburi Camp 1942/3

compounded this denial of opportunity to bring the Holy Sacraments to fellow Catholics. On one occasion a Christian Japanese doctor managed to procure some sacramental wine for him to celebrate Mass. A lot of the time was spent digging graves as well as conducting many burial services.

This unnecessary waste of young lives underpinned his resolve to build a church in suffrage to the memory of all those of whatever creed or faith who had died around him and in other camps … if he survived himself.

After his release, both from captivity and the Army, the Bishop of Northampton sent him to Wymondham's tiny Mission church with its growing congregation on a permanent site that needed developing. It was just the opportunity Fr. Cowin was looking for: here he could fulfil the vow he had made in adversity. While Norfolk might not be an obvious choice for such a memorial, it has very strong reasons for being the right place for it. Alongside other East Anglian Regiments, many units of the 18th Division that became FEPOW were Territorial Battalions from Norfolk, Suffolk and Cambridgeshire. His vision was to create a traditional Parish Church where their memory would be constantly revitalised by the prayers and worship of its faithful. In this way it would reach beyond barren granite monoliths and be a living memorial

But Wymondham was still a 'Poor Mission' and his other Mass centres, Attleborough and Dereham, also had to be served. Post-war austerity and its shortages had to be managed, and Wymondham with Dereham district had to be reorganised to make best use of his time and petrol ration. Across his district Masses, catechism classes and Confession timings were changed considerably.

In this early post–war period, it is easy to forget that Britain still had foreign POWs in East Anglia some until as late as 1948. Amongst them, locally, were German Catholics attending the little Stable Church. Fr. Cowin's Mass schedule was very tight, and two weeks after Easter he raised the possibility for Attleborough's Catholics that Mass would have to be stopped; this time not through lack of support as had been the case in Fr. Phillips time.

Since the end of March, additional to the POWs, some of the first students from Morley College had joined his congregation. When the last Mass in Attleborough was announced the following week, on April 27th, the bitter pill of their loss of facility was sweetened by the provision of regular transport to Mass at Wymondham.

His ideas for a new church had been mentioned to all his congregations, and March 23rd saw his first article appear in 'The Universe' announcing his plans to a wider audience. Further articles and publicity followed. By the second anniversary of the Japanese surrender, 15th August 1947, with the authoritative support of his Bishop and credibility of aristocratic patronage, his public subscription scheme, was launched in the Catholic, local and national press. The Mission Book records the event on August 24th, mentioning the figure needed for the first time - £15,000.

He reminded them again at the end of September that *'... every week until the Church is built I am offering Mass for their Spiritual and Temporal welfare.'*

Fr. Cowin wrote hundreds of letters to bereaved spouses, parents and relatives of FEPOW on casualty lists notified to the Commonwealth War Graves Commission. They were invited to donate money towards the church. In return, he would offer Mass daily for their souls and when it was built, send them an 'In Memoriam' photograph card of the new church with the name of their deceased FEPOW inscribed inside. Eventually, their names would be inscribed in a Book of Remembrance.

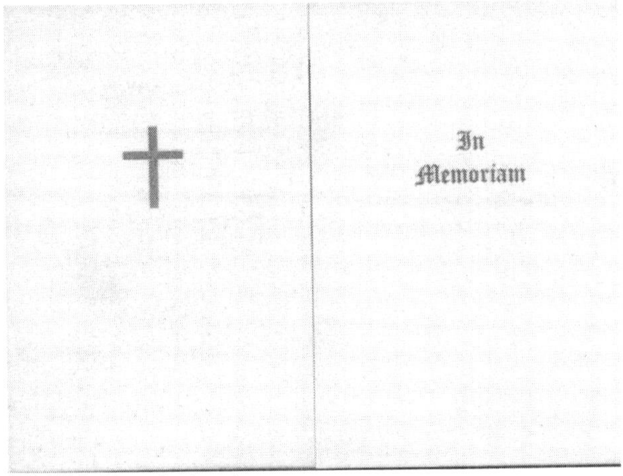

FEPOW 'In Memoriam' card

Another legacy of Norfolk's supportive wartime American 'occupation' was the collection of Nissen Huts, large and small, built up at the behest of the Ministry of Works on the Mid Norfolk golf course adjacent to Morley Hall. This land, originally requisitioned for food production at the outbreak of war, was turned into an Emergency Military Hospital run by the Americans for their troops and casualties in September 1943. On repatriation, effective midnight 8th June 1945, 231st Station Hospital was vacated. As War Ministry property it was briefly used as a transit camp for troops until 1946 when the Ministry of Works gave the site a new purpose under the auspices of the Ministry of Education as Wymondham Emergency Training College for Teachers. Students arrived there from April 1947 and The Roman Catholic Society, as members of the Student Christian Movement, became involved in many dance socials and other events to raise funds towards the planned Memorial Church, as well as making some items of church furniture for the Mission Church, such as candlesticks. By March 1948 he was making weekly visits to Morley Hall to say Mass and give spiritual support. The students were also able to give him advance notice of

Nissen Huts being dismantled to make way for better student facilities in the grounds. As a temporary building its potential as a church hall and social centre for fund-raising was obvious and ideal. By a delightful irony, two 'small' ones were soon joined together in the orchard area of the church's site where our first resident priest had once said his office. The college was closed in June 1950, but Fr. Cowin still had a role to play there in providing Catholic students with spiritual support when the Department of Education refocused the college's remit on the provision of secondary education.

Yet another legacy of Allied wartime support also made for extra priestly work. Many Polish pilots had remained here post-war and some were housed locally at the Polish Hostel in Ellingham. To attend to their spiritual welfare, Fr. Cowin had to re-arrange his Thursday Mass schedule so he could say Mass there from 16th November.

The regular business of maintaining church necessities remained difficult for money was still tight in July 1947. To aid the Memorial Church Fund, a Repository shop- *'strictly cash!'* - was started, and also a *'Library – books on loan @ 3d a week run by Sidney Caddy'*. It also meant the reintroduction of the Altar Society envelope for Altar expenses. While attention here is focussed on money, we get an idea of how many were squeezed into the Stable Church when in January 1948 he was disheartened to find that out of an average congregation of 100, only 20 envelopes were returned. The limited capacity (75) meant that Advent preparations had to be practical as well as spiritual: Midnight Mass 1947 was an 'All Ticket event!' He had already chartered a bus for Attleborough Catholics to come to Midnight Mass. This necessary arrangement for Attleborough Catholics at Christmas was unfortunately followed in January by the enforced cancellation of one of the regular buses bringing them to Mass, because *'receipts are £10 down on payments. The cost can only be met if every seat is paid for.'* This left them with only the 10.30am bus for 11am Mass. In reviewing his accounts he had some small delight: the Memorial Church fund had reached £3011/11/4d! His Mass centres were now at Wymondham – Sunday Mass at 8am and 11am; and 9.30am at Dereham.

It was a reasonable expectation that parishioners would be willing to help raise funds. An informal CWL section had previously started up in 1933 but lapsed during the war. Fr. Cowin foresaw that if he could harness their industriousness within an organised group, they could play a valuable role in the parish. On the evening of Sunday 11th April 1948 Fr. Cowin invited the ladies of the church to meet with him in the Presbytery after Mass as he had an *'announcement of considerable interest to them which will offer full scope for their activities….'* Sixteen brave ladies came forward and after hearing how the Catholic Women's League had benefitted other parishes and The Church, they agreed to form a section. It was formally set up at their first meeting on 20th April with Mrs Mary Gaynor elected as its first president. With no space for them to meet, the Presbytery was offered - fortnightly on Tuesday afternoons - until the Nissen Hut he had just acquired to be used as a hall was installed and fitted out. It was 6 months before it was ready, but at last, after evening Mass on October 31st, Fr. Cowin invited all parishioners to see inside their new church hall. It was open to parishioners only for light refreshments and dancing between 7 and 10pm with an assurance for Attleborough folk that they would not be turned out in the cold until it was time for the bus to depart! It became a regular feature with tickets for dancing charged at 1 shilling

Evidently 1948 was already turning out to be a significant year. Since the restoration of Our Lady's Shrine at Walsingham in 1897 and the great public Pilgrimage of 1934 led by Cardinal Bourne and Bishop Youens, it had become a focus for pilgrimage. Amongst the first Cross Carrying Pilgrimages was the post-war Student Cross Pilgrimage for Peace, Penance and Prayer. The Essex Leg started from Colchester in that July and Wymondham's Mission Church was one of its last overnight stops *en route* to Walsingham. Their arrival on the 13th July was hosted by the ladies of the recently formed CWL section who were on hand to provide sustenance to the weary foot pilgrims. Nowadays, the Student Cross Pilgrimage takes place during Lent, and by tradition the Lent Walkers arrive on the Wednesday of Holy Week. Set by the CWL then, it has continued every year to the present day except for 2001 when BSE restrictions forced them to abandon it.

The Nissen Hut Hall, which had cost £370, was finally pressed into service for its first money-raising venture a few months later, on December 15th 1948 when the CWL held a Sale of Work. It realised the excellent sum of £25 (equivalent to about £700 in 2012). This amount, with some other donations and smaller scale efforts went towards paying off the debt, allowing Fr. Cowin to reduce it by £100.

Monies raised thereafter went towards reducing this debt further as well as raising funds for the new church. Since then, the CWL has funded many other things, including payment of some utility bills as well as church furnishings: a font, vestments' repairs, altar linen and more recently the vertical blinds on the Sanctuary windows.

When advance notice of the next Sale of Work in 1949 was given out and the phenomenon of the Jumble Sale appeared! Fr. Cowin's dream was a little closer to reality. Fund-raising had taken off, there was public support for the new church and parishioners had become a cohesive community with a common purpose. Apart from the perennial problem of income generation - Altar Society envelopes returned from only a quarter of the congregation, and the church expenses in deficit - the practicalities of parish life: Masses, Confessions, Catechism and Confirmation classes all seemed to have assumed an air of permanence. The next generation of Catholics was being nurtured, bolstered by his encouragement of children's Christmas parties' and outings to the seaside all under the auspices of the CWL.

By June 1949 the Memorial Church Fund stood at almost £4,500, and Fr. Cowin was able to announce *'commencement of building next Spring. Need to increase the fund to at least £6000 - another £1500'.* The request for volunteer labour to clear the site of trees in advance of the building work came shortly afterwards – just two hours a week!

A major social event was organised - a huge Dance and Social held at the Women's Institute Hall, (demolished in 1950s) on the 26th October with local celebrities in attendance: sporting heroes of Norwich City Football Club - 1st team players and their manager; a team of local Cricket Players (including several County players) It made £250. Following on that success The Allied POW Memorial Building Club with a monthly prize draw of £75 (maximum membership 1000) was set up in the March of 1950. This proved equally successful. By the end of April with 675 members it had taken the fund over £5000.

Fr. Cowin, justifiably claimed that during his tenure he had built three churches in his area: Diss, Dereham and Wymondham. Although Mission Book entries give scant mention to his spiritual care in Diss, despite overseeing the building of their church, his emphasis on prayer is clear especially for Dereham Catholics who were also raising money for a new church. Just as the power of fervent prayer in 1926 provided Wymondham's Catholics with a resident priest, in January 1949 Fr. Cowin pressed his 'flock' gathered in Dereham to say *'6000 Hail Mary's - 50 per week from 30 people - each month for speedy erection of new church.'*

The fund-raising continued throughout 1950 and it must have been Dereham that prayed with greater fervour, as notification that building their new church could begin was announced on November 14th, and its current church opened and blessed on

23rd September 1951. It was a joyful bonus for them that Fr. Cowin arranged to say Midnight Mass there in consecutive years, leaving Wymondham with two Christmas Day Masses at 8am and 11am. Midnight Mass would return there when the new church had been built.

The New Church

Funding a new church build in post-war austerity was as economically difficult for Wymondham's Mission Church as physically constructing three Chapels in the jungle. Fr. Cowin's original grandiose design included a bell tower, two Sacristies and two side-Chapels: one to Our Lady and a Memorial Chapel. A local architect Donovan Purcell - a parishioner and previously Surveyor to the Fabric of Ely Cathedral, came up with the final design which also catered for the possibility of being extended at a later date.

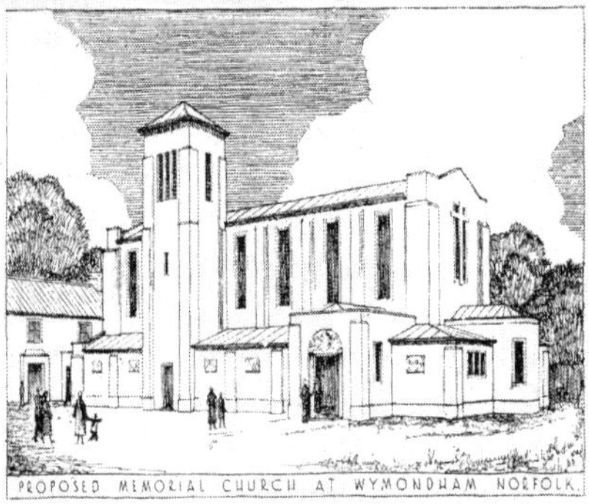

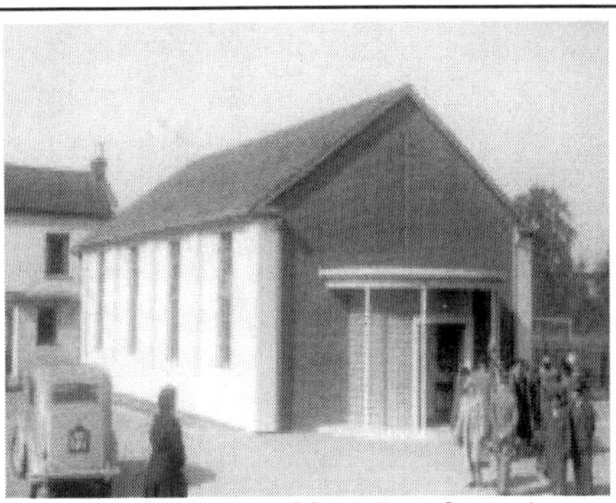

Our Lady & St. Thomas of Canterbury September 1952
(Original Semi-circular Portico)

It seated 150 and was completed in 1952. But by October 1951 when building started it had become clear that donations would not achieve the desired target of £15,000. Drastic economies in the scale of its design and construction followed swiftly when its projected cost had to be halved. The compromise arrived at was minimalist of necessity and had little adornment: the side-chapel to Our Lady was retained and the main body of the church became the 'Memorial Chapel' with a reredos reminiscent of that erected in its Anglican neighbour. As in captivity, only the tenacity to see it through remained intact. By happy coincidence this enforced simplicity made for greater resonance symbolically with the impoverished circumstances and scarcity of resources experienced in captivity. Externally, it had a lightweight roof of Western Red Cedar shingle tiles rather than the heavier traditional pan-tiles, modern long metal-framed single-glazed windows and inset in its gable end a Cross of glass bricks. When the church was lit the illuminated Cross would proclaim Our Lord's presence to all who passed by, and in that action be evidence of the 'living' element of the memorial he had intended. Uniquely, the entrance also featured a surround of the same glass bricks, and a semi-circular portico supported by four pillars.

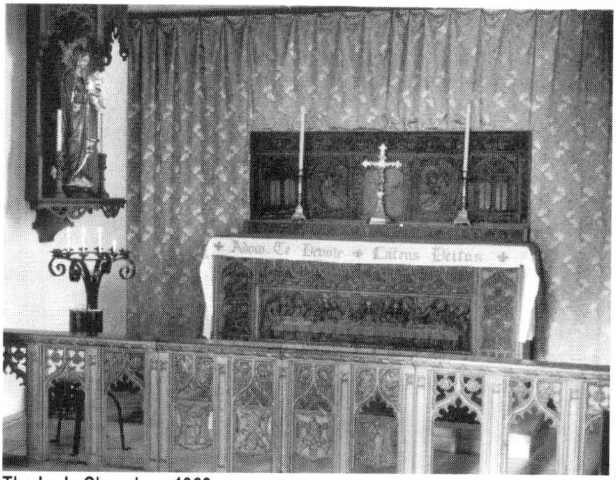

The Lady Chapel ca.1960

Internally, the old was blended with the new and its seating was individual chairs. English and oriental woods were used symbolically for its pulpit, half-panelled Sanctuary and painted reredos complementing in understatement the church's simplicity. The heritage oak carved Altar which was too small for the new church, and the carved oak Altar rail, also originating from the Town Green and Stable Churches, found their places reserved in The Lady Chapel which was set up for devotional worship. Unhappily, the rail was cut down to fit between the brick piers of the Lady Chapel, and was not restored until it was re-designated a Memorial Chapel and FEPOW shrine. Arguably, other items needed for the new church were an altar crucifix and the Altar itself. It was some three months after building had started that these two important items and the reredos were gifted anonymously. This unassuming parishioner and munificent benefactor had remained unknown until recently and can now be gratefully named as Dr G.C. Gaynor. The magnificent new Altar, by Messrs. Saunders of Ipswich, is of Portland stone with an incised and gilded Cross and Crown of Thorns on its front panel; and the Sanctuary was bounded by a modern wrought iron balustrade. It was Fr. Cowin's inspiration to have 24 saintly martyrs around Christ enthroned and his angelic supporters with 6 diaper pattern panels. The reredos was painted by the Cambridge artist John Hensher and has 35 painted sycamore panels. He later added four of the forty martyrs who were canonised in 1970 to the bottom row.

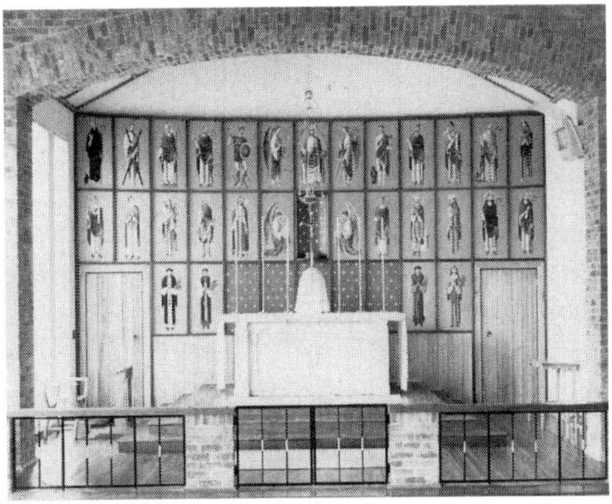

Sanctuary 1952

In preparation for the move into the new building, from Easter Sunday (April 13th) onwards, the Stable Church relinquished its service to Our Lord and was returned to its former purpose of storage, and Mass was said in the Hall. Once the date for the opening service was set in early July *'the Foreman had instructions to refuse admission to casual viewers'* of the new church. Amongst the many preparations for the great day was the provision of tickets to attend the opening ceremony – they had to be applied for, although Miss Adelaide Cross, as 'Founder of the Faith', received her invitation from Fr. Cowin;

and from July 24th, weekly rehearsals for a mixed choir led by Mr Purcell were started in preparation for the sung High Mass at the opening ceremony. But their ad hoc choral line-up lacked the confidence of practised choristers and was augmented by the choir from St John's, Norwich. A wry note was added to the notices for the Altar boys coming from Attleborough as he warned that they *'may be late home for dinner on that day'!* They were also reminded that as Benediction and Evening service resumed they would again be required to attend. The final ceremony of the day Erecting the Stations of the Cross would follow at 3pm when the Blessed Sacrament would be Blessed for the first time in the new church.

At the Bishop's insistence, the church's dedication to Our Lady and St Thomas of Canterbury was retained. This resonated contemporaneously with FEPOW in the Camps and re-connected the church with its local heritage historically. Although it would have to be consecrated at a later date, at 11am on Saturday September 20th, Fr. Cowin's solemn vow was finally fulfilled when his 'Living Memorial' to FEPOW was opened and Blessed by Rt.Rev Mgr. Canon McShee, VG, against the backdrop of its saintly reredos. Many brother priests, including Fr. Ketterer, joined the three other ex-FEPOW priests who concelebrated the profound and moving sung High Mass: Fr. J O'Mahoney CF; Fr. A Jackson OFM and Fr. P Rorke. Another priest, Fr. J Bebb who had taken Holy Orders after captivity, assisted. Now that the church was completed, the promised 'In Memoriam' Cards were on sale at 2/6d with profits going towards the New Church Fund.

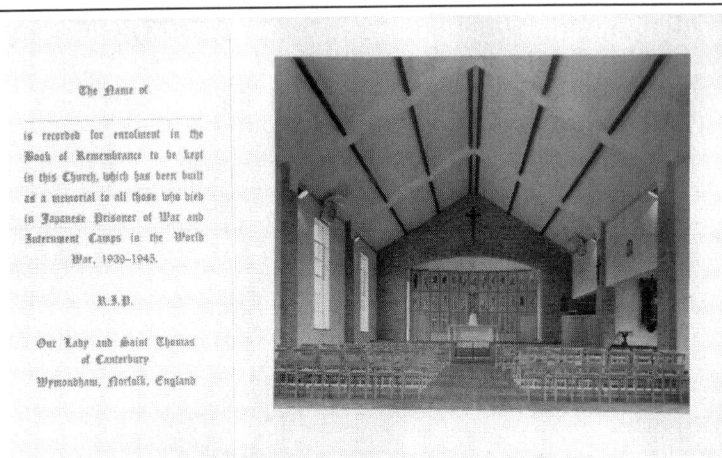

The Name of

is recorded for enrolment in the Book of Remembrance to be kept in this Church, which has been built as a memorial to all those who died in Japanese Prisoner of War and Internment Camps in the World War, 1939-1945.

R.I.P.

Our Lady and Saint Thomas of Canterbury

Wymondham, Norfolk, England

'In Memoriam; Card for FEPOW

There was no question where Midnight Mass was going to be celebrated this year! But Dereham parishioners were given advance notice at the beginning of November that a coach would be hired for them, in addition to the one for his Attleborough flock.

The future of any community is dependent on its youth, and the Altar boys who had proved themselves so capable at the opening ceremony continued to be diligent in serving The Lord at Sunday Mass, including Benediction over the next few years. To formalise their ministry Fr. Cowin set up a branch of the Archconfraternity of St Stephen – a boys only group – the Altar Servers Guild. The solemn and impressive enrolment ceremony should have been in time for Christmas 1955 but an outbreak of Polio at Wymondham College, where a number of boys were pupils, caused it to be postponed due to quarantine restrictions. It finally took place on Palm Sunday afternoon 1956. It was an unfortunate irony that having devoted much energy towards getting his Altar Servers enrolled, he was unable to fulfil the Holy Week liturgy in full as substantial changes to the rubrics came into force and he was not allowed to perform them in part. However, two years later on Palm Sunday 1958, to keep abreast of the social changes in the wider community, he obtained the Bishop's permission to set up a similar ministry for the girls – The Guild of St. Agnes. As a junior branch of the Children of Mary, they too had their own regalia – a white veil and a scarlet shoulder cloak and medallion on a red ribbon. It mixed religion and fun for girls. On certain days they processed and took part in the Mass, and their social activities included: singing, dancing, sewing and other useful household skills. One mundane task they took on was maintaining the polished patina of the church brassware – not a job for the faint-hearted as there were ten candlesticks and the Altar crucifix! It was 1996 before girls were allowed to serve Our Lord at the Altar, when Claire Wiseman and Claire Engler became trailblazers in Wymondham.

With building finished, the church that Fr. Cowin's ceaseless drive had built had cost almost £10,000 including all furnishings. It had been paid for by the generous public subscriptions of over 2000 people, many non-Catholics, donations of beneficent parishioners, many of whom remained anonymous, and the unstinting fund-raising of its Catholic community. At his visitation in 1953, the Bishop had promised to donate the last £50 of the debt. As a 'Christmas present' in 1956, he did so. This finally enabled the enlarged car-park we have today to be finished and the church re-decorated outside. From conception to completion it had taken 5 years, and a further 4 years to pay off the debt.

SAINTS ON THE REREDOS - 1952

Benedict	Andrew	David	Patrick	George	Archangel Gabriel	Christ in Glory	Archangel Michael	John the Evangelist	Denis	Gregory	Giles	Francis
Augustine	Alban	Etheldreda	Edmund	Thomas Becket	Angel with Ciborum	Diaper Pattern	Angel with Chalice	Fursey	Ethelbert	Wythburga	Aidan	Columba
Panelled Door		Edmund Campion	John Fisher	Diaper Pattern *	Diaper Pattern *	Diaper Pattern	Diaper Pattern *	Diaper Pattern *	Thomas More	Margaret Clitheroe	Panelled Door	
		Scalloped Panelling										

Saints on the Reredos 1952

Only one thing remained to fully complete his vow: The Book of Remembrance. It had been an integral part of the publicity and information while the funds were raised and the church built. In the interim, he and his friend, ex-FEPOW Frank Hardy, had researched methods and materials for inscribing names of their fallen comrades into 'Honour Rolls'. It was a very involved task and he had no previous experience. In brief, they agreed to collect the names from private sources as well as War Department Casualty lists and the Commonwealth War Graves Commission; and Frank would collate, arrange and inscribe them. For the book a 200gm cream paper – 'goatskin parchment' – was chosen and the cover was to be deep blue goatskin leather. A customised block was made replicating his own unique cursive script to impress a title on the spine of each Book, and machine tooled lines representing the sun's rays coming diagonally from the top corners so that they crossed over on the spine of the Book. The symbolism is unmistakable. In terms of their organisation, the Books of Remembrance were not numbered so that no one book has precedence over another. But as by far the greatest numbers of FEPOW were British Army, the first Book started with their names. However, practicality required them to be entered alphabetically, with conventional Service and Regimental precedence ignored, although force of military habit meant that officers preceded the rank and file.

Simply put, there were to be 25 names on the page showing Number, Rank, Surname, Initials and Unit on a single line. After much experimentation, he devised a spacing that avoided focussing on the service number and allowing the person's name to be centred on that line. Specimen pages were displayed in the new church, and donors sought to subscribe to the approximate cost of £200 for 3 volumes containing some 25,000 names. The collation was time consuming, with lists often being adjusted, but he finally made a start on entering the names in late 1958. It was late January 1960 before the first volume –British Army A-O – was handed over to Fr. Cowin, with a second volume following quickly in

September 1960 - remaining British and Commonwealth Forces. The last volume, Dutch Forces and Civilians, took much longer and was not delivered until December 1962. There was of course no point in having these Books unless they were on show. A local craftsman, Mr W.G. Filby, was engaged to make a display cabinet of light English Oak with an internal electric light to illuminate the Books when completed. It would also have a panelled triptych with scriptural texts inscribed on three bronze plates ... for which more donations would be sought. It was situated at the back of the church beside the entrance for the next 40 years so that people could affirm the memory of those enshrined within as they passed by. There it remained until continuing growth of the congregation caused the current Narthex to be built in the Millennium year. By this time the Lady Chapel had gone out of use as a devotional chapel and was redundant for worship. The inspiration of another priest was to return it to a former intention; that of a Memorial Chapel, and recreate it as a shrine for the display cabinet and the Books of Remembrance within the Memorial Church. It also provided the opportunity to restore the oak Altar Rail, and conserve the oak Altar, both carved by Cecil Cross over 50 years ago. The side-chapel was refurbished and the display cabinet's triptych of bronze plaques replaced by three freestanding beech plinths supporting a modern triptych of engraved Perspex with its scriptural texts in the twentieth century version. The display cabinet, originally a light oak, was stained to match the 1929 Altar Rail colour. An eternal flame burns in their memory. Although this was a significant positional reordering, the FEPOW shrine is an integral part of the Church which is itself the memorial and Fr. Cowin said Mass each day for the War dead until he left the parish in August 1965.

It is often the case that external factors can take the shine off a major milestone. For not only had the debt been cleared, and Wymondham had a record attendance at Midnight Mass, but petrol rationing that was still in force left him unable to fulfil all the Christmas duties at Dereham – the furthest extremity of his area.

Over the years all conceivable methods of fund-raising had been pressed into servicing the church debt. Donations, covenants and the 'lottery style' New Church Building Club continued, Church Fund Collecting Boxes, collections outside church; Whist Drives, Grand Draws and Raffles, Dance Socials, Jumble Sales, Bring & Buy Sales and Sales of Work. In addition the CWL organised the first of many Christmas Fairs on December 11th 1954. It was most successful, raising £62. The children were not left out either as they collected 'ship' halfpennies in the hope of winning a model of the 'Golden Hinde. Collectors were also organised to visit parishioners in house to house collections at one stage. By June 1956 the church debt stood at just under £150, although that did not take account of the interest charges which were $^{1}/_{3}$ of that figure.

But however fervent the prayer and worship of this community, the financial glue needed reinventing. A new, and novel, form of fund-raising caught the football fever of its time: Football Pools by subscription were introduced on 17th February 1957. People subscribed and received codes corresponding to football teams which were checked against published match results each week, with winning codes announced in the Bulletin. It turned out to be very successful, just as another pressing need became apparent. A new hall was needed. As a social and fund-raising centre the Nissen Hut had been a functional success but it lacked facilities and was cold in the winter. The continuing need for housing ten years post-war had been temporarily eased by the Arcon prefabricated house unit designed by the Ministry of Works. Fr. Cowin saw that the facilities of two units joined together could serve equally as well as a Church Hall. And it did. The result was a modern, functional space with kitchen facilities and flush sanitation too. This much bigger building had a small Guild Room for meetings, and a larger space for parochial and social functions with the latest infra-red wall heaters. Apart from its erection, the prefabricated shell was fitted out and decorated by local craftsmen, and a parishioner, Sidney Caddy, created a picturesque garden pond feature in a corner of the main room. Other 'modern' features were a switchboard to control the heaters, and a record player for music to dance to on the oak parquet dance floor. It was opened and Blessed by Canon G Roberts from St. Johns, Norwich on September 25th 1957. He returned a few days later to Bless a new 'Martinette' electric organ which replaced the harmonium that had been transferred from the stable church; an anonymous gift from two parishioners. Just before the next football season started in July 1960, he was pressing for more subscribers and collectors for the Pools. In 3½ years it had raised over £4,600 and one of its spectacular outcomes was the recently acquired hall.

Liturgically, Mass was still being said in the Tridentine format and heard by the congregation with only the Altar Servers making the Latin responses to the priest's invocations. To accommodate post-war social awareness the Mass had to evolve. Priestly rubrics had changed in1956 and a few years later, in 1959, the Holy Father directed that the laity were to participate more fully in the Mass and the Dialogue Mass was introduced. Here parishioners responded quite well to the instruction/practising of pronunciation and gave Fr. Cowin encouragement. They were well practised by the time of the Bishop's triennial visitation in May 1960 when he also confirmed 7 adults and 54 children from the Wymondham and Dereham area, including several members of the Guild of St Agnes. For Fr. Cowin it was one occasion where he would claim the sin of pride in having *'baptised many, if not most, of those the Bishop confirmed.'*

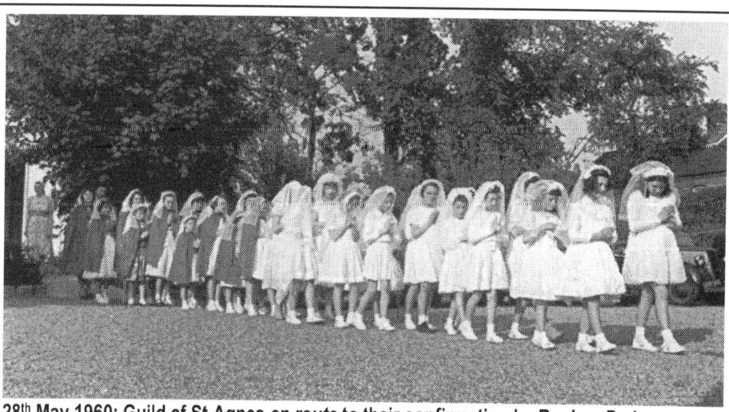

28th May 1960: Guild of St Agnes *en route* to their confirmation by Bp. Leo Parker

Fr. Cowin's designation was still Priest in Charge of two Poor Mission churches which were running quite well and its parishioners actively involved. But there was no let-up about insufficient offertories and other financial matters to both churches. He recounts that his most difficult task was reminding Wymondham parishioners that there was another church to look after in Dereham, and vice versa. Suffice to say that Dirham's constant plea for a priest of their own was addressed when in 1962 he embarked on a series of explanatory notes in the weekly bulletins, for both churches, about where the money went. This was another reason for parishioners to keep their bulletin. It did not assuage their feelings when the end result showed that both churches were still in deficit. In response to their pleadings, it was suggested that not enough income to maintain their own costs was a major reason for having to share a priest. And as if a portent of his tenure coming to an end, he followed it up with a comparison of average attendances and congregations. His Silver Jubilee as a priest the following year was well concealed from his parishioners, or so he thought, until the Bishop's visitation in June. To his surprise a presentation of a cheque for £54 was made at the celebratory tea after the Confirmation. His widowed mother had been acting as his housekeeper for a number of years, and in January 1965 she died. It was perhaps a contributory factor in his move to the Parish to St Joseph's College Ipswich on August 26th. As he reflected on his stay of 19 years, he put some 'mystic letters and numbers' in the bulletin: 8TKP 12JJK 19MLC. Parishioners worked it out the following week when he suggested they could add PP1962 after the last set. The puzzle was solved when he added DB2681965 (his successor) to the list. Clearly Wymondham had been relieved of its Poor Mission status at last and canonically recognised as a Parish in 1962. Strange to relate though, the date when this great milestone occurred is not recorded. From 1962-65 was also a momentous time for Catholics globally as the 2nd Vatican Council was in session. But its effects would not be brought into being by Wymondham's first Parish Priest. Fr. Cowin's incumbency had been a *tours de force* of priestly labour and the longest of any priest to date.

A Poor Mission No Longer

Having shaken off the shackles of being a 'Poor Mission' through 19 years of unremitting developmental drive, its community was somewhat fatigued and the Parish now needed the restorative effects of consolidation. However, acquisition of Parish status never promised magical solutions to the provision of financial support and neither was its pastor absolved from the need to remind his parishioners that their giving was not keeping pace with external fiscal pressures. But the relentless monetary demand was replaced by a less intense Pastoral request to make things better, as the next Parish Priest, Fr. Denis Brophy, had more subtle persuasions to employ. He had been chaplain to the Carmelite Convent at Quidenham whilst also looking after Diss' Catholics as Priest in Charge for 10 years. So it might be considered that his character building experience of being expelled as an 'undesirable alien' during his priestly training at Innsbruck in 1938 and his spiritual care as Pastor to the Nuns may have found him well placed for this incumbency. Neither did he have far to travel to take up his new appointment. But his move coincided with his annual departure to Lourdes with the Diocesan Pilgrimage, where he ministered to sick Pilgrims for many years, and the parish was left in the care of the Housekeeper, his overpowering pet Alsatian and a visiting Dominican Priest for that week.

It had fallen to Fr. Brophy to implement locally the changes stemming from the 2nd Vatican Council decisions. Many of them took time to filter through to Parish level with some taking longer than others to be introduced. From March 1965 some changes to the Mass were evidence of liturgical renewal taking place. A significant change governing attendance at Mass came into force almost immediately after the Council's conclusion. The rule that disallowed Catholics to attend was ameliorated and took effect in time for Remembrance Day 1965. Fr. Brophy was able to announce, *'Our Catholic people may now join in the Armistice Day celebrations and the civic services held in our towns'.* However, as in previous years, a Requiem Mass for the repose of the souls of the War Dead was held that evening as Catholics were still required to attend Mass on Sundays. With one major result from Vatican II evident, over the course of the next few years Fr. Brophy provided 'potted' explanations of some of its aspects in the weekly church notices. On April 24th 1966 another important element of change was that *'… the laity must play their part in the mission of the whole people of God in the church and in the world….'*

The properties of 'a cup of tea' are legion: notably restorative, but also facilitative and encouraging. As part of the laity's involvement on April 30th 1967 the CWL were asked to try a 'New Experiment' aiming to give an opportunity to meet fellow parishioners and newcomers through the sharing of refreshments after morning Mass on Sundays, as well as providing refreshment for those who came from a distance to the church. Its success has developed into a regular feature in the parish to the present day where a spin-off has been a fund-raising function too. Now members from the community take turns to provide this very important function as well as the CWL continuing to take their turn. The ladies involvement then was well established through the CWL and had shown financially tangible results. Their two Jumble Sales a year and Christmas Bazaar, now an annual event, were major sources of funds for the parish coffers. With a huge electric bill expected at the beginning of that December, Fr. Brophy reminded the faithful *'to support this wonderful institution by providing items and buying other ones back!'* Meanwhile the men's contribution had not yet been developed as an organised body, but an opportunity was expressed on Jan 9th 1966 by Mr Cramer of Wymondham with the idea to form a council of the Knights of St Columba. It did take off in 1967, but only as a satellite of Council 286 which was based in Norwich. In effect it complemented the work of the ladies but by 1974 was looking for more members. As a parish community shares its joys with its priest so, on September 18th 1966, did their priest share with them his joy when he was unexpectedly honoured. Bishop Grant was delegated to present him with the silver medal of the Hospitalité in charge of the sick Pilgrims to Lourdes. With the other silver medallists, including Bishop Grant, the Diocese of Northampton was distinguished by its service to the sick at Lourdes.

And yet barely a month later, on Feb 26th 1967, in common with all his predecessors, this Parish Priest also had to point out the inadequacies of the weekly offertory. He posed the question, *'How does 3/6d compare with what you gainfully earn for two hours work?'* to his congregations (Wymondham190 and Dereham 100) as the weekly collection was drifting again towards unsustainable levels. While the 'Pools' collectors successfully operated Fr. Cowin's maxim of utilising 'OPM' from members outside the church - nearly £9 a week - it underlined that our own congregations were not really supporting their parish. It was a sad irony that this fact had to be mentioned just a week after Dr George C Gaynor MC, one of this church's most generous benefactors, and supporter of the Parish since his arrival in Wymondham in 1919, had been laid to rest.

Another aspect of Vatican II was the call for Christian Unity. Halfway through January 1967 Christian bodies were prompted to actively seek and pray for Unity in the Church. Locally Fr. Brophy's outward looking support for fostering the Ecumenical movement and furthering Christian Aid became evident. One of the early events, organised by the youth of the Congregational Church on 18th November, used the defiant idea prevalent in the sixties of the 'Sit In' - a 'Starve-In'! As a staunch supporter of Church Unity and Christian Aid, Fr. Brophy urged his parishioners to attend this public event in the Market Place like a 'Family Fast Day'. The token gesture was *'to go without lunch and replace it with 'a bun and cup of coffee'* for just 3/-. A novel means of raising awareness and funds for the undernourished in the world, as a forerunner to bigger events.

Attleborough Catholics had been left without any local Masses since 1947 because of time pressures for Fr. Cowin's ministrations elsewhere and petrol rationing. Twenty years hence their numbers had increased significantly and Fr. Brophy came to an arrangement with The 'Travelling Missions', who still returned annually, to start a regular quarterly Mass there with Fr. R McCormick in St Mary's Church Hall on 6th August. Catechism numbers, for children, in Attleborough steadily grew and Fr. Brophy's gratitude was expressed when in 1971 Mr and Mrs Bennet's large front room became unavailable and a different venue had to be found. The quarterly Mass continued for several years until weekly Mass was able to restart after 1st October 1973 when his responsibility for Dereham was taken over by Swaffham Parish under the care of Fr. Anthony Sketch. Mass was once again said in Attleborough by Wymondham's Parish Priest. This redistribution of workload was evened out however on 2nd February 1974 when Mass was also recommenced at RAF Station Watton.

Encouraged by the response from the laity some additional changes in the Mass were ordered by authority of the Pope on Thursday, June 29th 1967. The Canon of the Mass was to be said aloud; and by July the Bishops were being asked to *'seek diverse opinion'* on many other aspects of the changes. Christmas 1967 saw the obligation of Fasting and Abstinence dispensed in advance of January 1st 1968 which finally rescinded the obligation of Fasting and Abstinence on Holy Days leaving Catholics everywhere to take the whole responsibility of penance themselves with guidance from their Parish Priest in the weekly Bulletin. Then, during Lent 1968 one of the most far reaching of Vatican II's changes was set in motion: the setting up of a Parish Council. The process was consultative with a general meeting of the Parish called on 12th March to discuss what it should do; how representative it should be, what offices should be provided and other implications. With such a wide parish to cover, Fr. Brophy had two to oversee, and a similar meeting took place at Dereham at the other end of the Parish. A provisional committee to deliberate further met on March 26th and its results reported on May 14th when 18 members, with one representing Dereham, were elected to serve for one year. It was timely that the Parish council should be in place as the church was frequently filled to its capacity of 150 and one of the new Parish Council's early tasks was to set in process plans to see how the church might be enlarged.

With the Parish Council in place, amongst its other considerations was how to involve the young people in the parish and help maintain their contact with the church. A meeting was organised for 25th May 1969 to determine how to get them together to support each other and see what they could be doing in the parish. A month later the young people themselves were invited along for them to decide, and from that, Our Lord's former house was relieved of storage duties and given renewed purpose to become a meeting place for them as 'The Stable Youth Club'. Various outings and fund raising activities followed until at least 1978.

Plans for extending and altering the church had been submitted to the Local Authority in January 1969,and received final approval in November 1970. But as Fr. Brophy explained to the local press, the work, by Mr P Hawkins (a parishioner) scheduled to take 12 weeks, would have to wait until after Christmas. When completed, the capacity of the church would be increased by 50-60, allowing six extra rows of seats. But it would involve some major changes internally as well as constructing a new and larger porch area which would provide a 'Cry Room', storage space and that very modern necessity, a toilet facility. The pulpit of oriental wood unfortunately took up valuable space and was removed; besides it was no longer considered fashionable. The Sanctuary too was not immune from change either as it was opened up with the removal of its familiar communion rail, and the polished quarry tiled floor covered with a low level carpeted dais to elevate the Altar. To keep the area around the Sanctuary clear it was necessary to relocate the organ console to the opposite corner at the back of the church where the Baptistery had been. This in turn was temporarily situated in the Lady Chapel. Moves on the Sanctuary also finally fulfilled another of Vatican II's changes; that of the priest facing the Faithful to celebrate the Mass. Messrs. A.J. Woods and Sons of Norwich carried out the work on the Altar and created an apse in the reredos wall beneath Christ enthroned for the Tabernacle. This higher position meant that steps had to be built so that the priest was able to reach the reserved Host, and the Eternal Flame formerly above the Altar re-sited to the South Wall as it would obscure the reserved place of Our Lord. All the alterations, necessitated by an increasing congregation, which had started in January 1971, were completed by Easter. Their timing usefully provided the impetus to address another momentous occasion in the Church. Some 6 months earlier on October 25th 1970, the Holy Father had Canonised the 40 Holy Martyrs of England and Wales. This had implications for the reredos, as the 4 beatified martyrs depicted on the bottom row needed to have their status changed. The recent internal work on the Sanctuary had also left the reredos looking incomplete, and Tom McCarten, a local artist , was asked to signify their new status and add 4 Norfolk Saints from those martyrs recently canonised to the gallery in place of 4 the 5 patterned panels, previously a backdrop for the Altar Candlesticks. As the panels were replaced, their order was changed to that which is visible today, but the reason for the rearrangement, if any, is not known.

SAINTS ON THE REREDOS - 1971

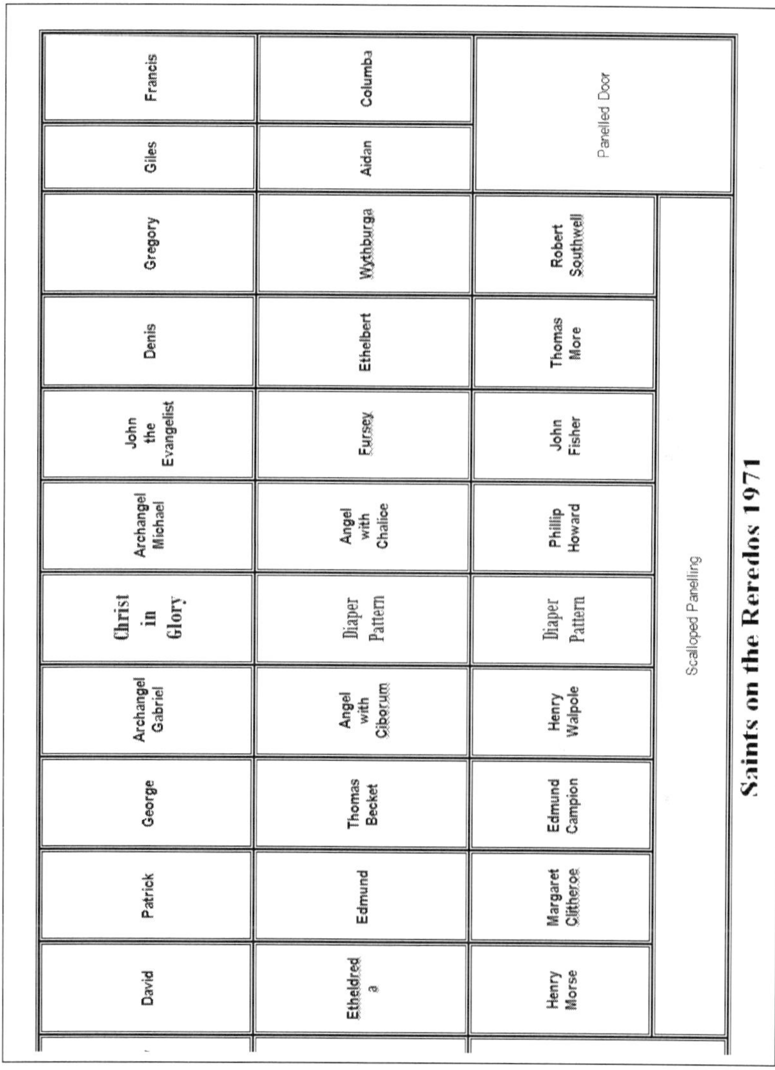

Saints on the Reredos 1971

As an active supporter of ecumenism and Christian Unity, Fr. Brophy's outward looking approach not only led him to represent the Diocese on these matters, but also to become Chairman of the Councils' of Churches in both Wymondham and Dereham. He was held in such regard, that in the service he led for Christian Unity on January 13th 1972 he showed just how forward looking Wymondham's Catholics were, when the Abbey Curate, Rev John Bliss was invited to be the first Anglican priest to preach in its Catholic church; and in the December, this same priest chose to be inducted as President of Wymondham's Council of Churches in this church. It is unsurprising that ecumenism percolated into Parish life.

It was also in this year that the challenge of Catechism Camps for children which had been so successful elsewhere in the Northampton Diocese for some time was promoted by Wymondham's CWL. Mrs Carol Donnelly sought applications from April 1972 and for the East Anglian camps starting in early August at Walsingham and Lowestoft. Aimed, originally, at children aged 7-11 years who did not attend Catholic schools, it was an opportunity to mix fun with religion. A holiday and instruction combined for £6 - it was good value. Many children from Wymondham Parish have enjoyed great benefits from them on all levels over the years. The connection continues with financial and practical help from them to the present day. Nationally, in 1998/9, the CWL Camps were faced with implementing Child Protection Legislation. The costs associated with this and increasing insurance premiums threatened their continuation. However, in East Anglia Bishop Peter Smith saw the value of the Camps and agreed to give them financial support, promoting them as East Anglia Diocesan Summer Camps.

The Catholic population in Wymondham and Dereham had grown significantly in this time, fed by the tremendous increase in the surrounding populace. But Fr. Brophy's incumbency came to an end 10 years after leaving the Nuns at Quidenham, on 31st September 1975 when he was sent to the even larger parish of Felixstowe. With him too went his Housekeeper Mrs Penny Rigby, who had taken over from Miss Margaret Mooney when she retired some years earlier, and his other 'guardian', pet Alsatian Ruigh, (King in Gaelic). A deeply respected man and much loved priest, he had devoted considerable efforts towards teaching the children of his far flung parish, and overseen the changes wrought by Vatican II. The effectiveness of his ministry is shown by the transformation of his congregations locally, from an inwardly focussed spirituality to a more inclusive outward-looking Faith. He also had the unique distinction of being the only Priest President in the worldwide Rotarian Movement having been invited to join the Rotary Club in Wymondham in 1969. It would be his successor who would see this fully fledged Parish into a new diocese.

Diocese of East Anglia

1976

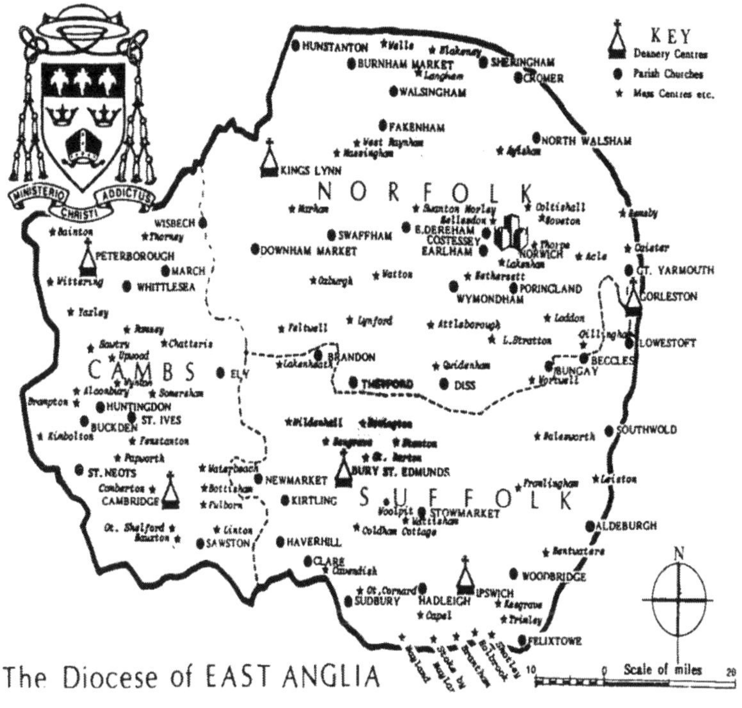

Diocese of East Anglia ca.1989

A New Parish in a New Diocese

The 1st October 1975 found Fr. Kenneth S Chapman, an East Anglian, travelling away from Aldeburgh in his native Suffolk to become Wymondham's third Parish Priest bringing his loyal Housekeeper Miss Dorothy Scarfe with him. His incumbency would be significant, not only as the last round of priestly moves directed by the Bishop of Northampton, but also as it was beset by major worries and ill health which made it his last move too.

Just eight short months after his arrival, on 2nd June 1976, he had the great joy of ushering the Parish into a new era within the newly created Diocese of East Anglia under Bishop Alan Clark. This historic development also gave Fr. Chapman the honour of securing the 1st Bishop of East Anglia's first engagement after his Episcopal Ordination: the Confirmation Mass for 48 candidates in a concelebrated ceremony with His Lordship and Canon McBride. To mark the occasion further, Wymondham's KSC provided them with a 'Guard of Honour' en route to a reception afterwards in the Parish Hall provided by the capable ladies of the CWL.

The laity were now actively involved in the church with many people regularly engaged and organised on Rotas for: Readers in the Mass, Offertory collectors, Altar procession, Flower arrangers and church cleaning – it was still a polished quarry –tiled floor. With Mass attendance at 175+ calls for a Mass centre to be set up in Hethersett were voiced and an Anticipatory Mass was commenced there during mid-1977 on Saturday evenings at 6pm; Summer in the Methodist Church and Winter in St Remegius Anglican Church. It nearly faltered, as attendance was low for a while, because St John's Cathedral in Norwich had also started a similar arrangement which may have distracted Hethersett's Catholics. Wymondham also continued the ecumenical activity fostered by Fr. Brophy and in the service of induction led by Fr. Chapman on April 15th, Mrs Carol Donnelly (RC) as outgoing

President of Wymondham Council of Churches handed over the Presidency to Rev G R Hall (The Abbey).

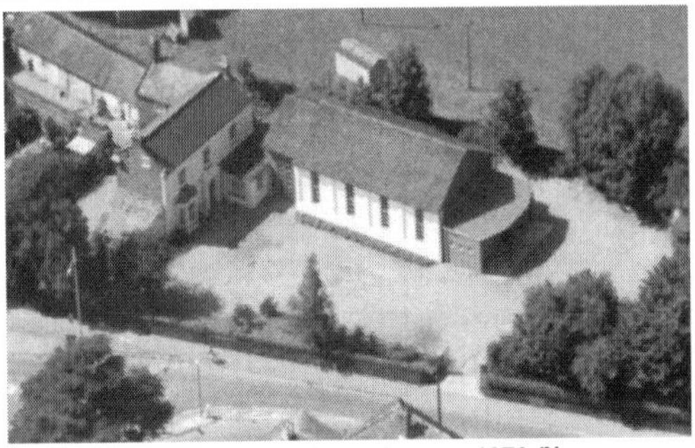
Our Lady & St. Thomas of Canterbury ca.1976 (New Porch1971)

The long, very hot Summer of '76 that greeted the new diocese was followed in 1977 by an atrocious winter which significantly reduced numbers at Mass for a few weeks. Despite some major design compromises made due to lack of funds when it was built, the 'Living Memorial' church had just celebrated its Silver Jubilee in the service of Our Lord that September. The first signs of trouble showed up a weakness in the durability of the Cedar-wood shingle-tiled roof when it developed a leak. Concern was such that a Roof Fund was started in January 1978 well in advance of any specialist inspection. Anxiety increased in October when news that Holy Apostles Catholic Church in West Earlham, Norwich (same age and identical roof), was having its roof replaced at a cost of £3800 due to similar problems. Fund raising in earnest was again in full swing: regular coffee after Sunday morning Mass, a KNIT-IN by the ladies with wool donated by parishioners, and scheme sponsoring BUY A TILE for 10p. Even children could help – a 'Smarties' tube was just the right size for 1p coins. The Christmas Bazaar, now a larger affair having outgrown the Parish Hall, was in the Town's Central Hall under a collective parochial 'task force'. It needed to make a good profit this year.

Fears about the roof were confirmed, and it had to be completely replaced, but it did not get the go-ahead until 1979. Scaffolding went up on June 14th but unseasonably bad weather delayed the start of repairs. The damage was extensive and challenging to repair because of its unique construction, but the skill of the Roofer and Builder, Mr P Hawkins, was able to achieve a very satisfactory result. The work was completed by July 15th 1979 for less than the anticipated £3200 cost. Fortunately, despite worries that there were insufficient goods, the Bazaar exceeded expectations by raising £574 and swelling the Roof Fund total to almost half the target figure.

A mature seminarian, Mr Joe Farrell, and former parishioner of Watton, was on leave from the Beda College Rome helped Fr. Chapman as Minister of the Eucharist in Watton as Fr. Chapman had developed some health concerns. The laity's involvement in this ministry to assist the priest *'should he be impeded'* came out of Vatican II. As a result, after training, two men, Mr Jim Murphy and Mr Barry Say, were commissioned by Canon McBride on 17th December 1978 as the first Special Ministers of the Eucharist in Wymondham.

Catholic congregations excuse for poor singing was always put down as a hangover from Penal Times when any musical strains could give-away a covert Mass. Fr. Chapman, renowned for his booming tones, was often disappointed by the volume his congregation produced for the hymns. It was sufficiently poor that year for him to request his flock to 'sing up' at Mass. Many of the tunes were considered old fashioned and popular music since the sixties had not really penetrated the Catholic Church, despite Churches elsewhere having used Folk Hymns and Folk Masses for several years. The trial inclusion of some Folk Hymns on August 12th was reported by Fr. Chapman in the Bulletin that they *'went well and it seemed to me that people were singing well'*. A folk music group was formed and practised together on the Saturday before Mass and played quarterly. Their first planned rendition in Mass was on October 14th 1979 and as the organist was away they also played at the Christmas Masses.

Whereas Abbot Howarth from Downside had helped Fr. Chapman for several years by saying Mass at Attleborough, by 4th May 1980 he had to stop due to ill health. The reins there had once again to be taken up by Fr. Chapman until the 'Autumn manoeuvres' of the clergy were known. In late August 1981 their care, and Wayland Hospital, was taken over by the priest who had spiritual care of the Quidenham Nuns. But this additional workload came at a bad time with more maintenance problems on top of the recent roof repairs. The stable wall facing the Kings Head Meadow suddenly showed that it too had suffered in that bad winter. Large holes in the pebbledash and several missing tiles were evident in mid-May, raising questions about whether it *'should be repaired, left to rot or be pulled down'*. In the end he decided that it was too unsafe and it was pulled down. These problems were compounded by vandalism and more difficulties were caused by children clambering over the rickety wooden boundary fence.

Some cracks in the church; which Fr. Cowin had said were there almost as soon as the church was built, had become obvious, and in September 1980 Fr. Chapman asked the Diocesan Surveyor to inspect the property. He expressed concern about them too, but thought that neither church nor property was likely to fall down. However, he would get a subsidence specialist to look at them. It was March 1981 before they visited the church to carry out their survey and investigations. The cost of repairs to the fence and other maintenance had just come through when Pynfords of Chelmsford sent him their report in August. It was an absolute disaster: the church was unsafe! Some remedial work was recommended to be done quickly and temporary shoring-up of the external church wall on the car-park side was put in place. Initial estimates suggested a cost of £20-25000 meant that this decision was for the Bishop and Diocesan Finance Board to say what work could be afforded, and they did not meet until September.

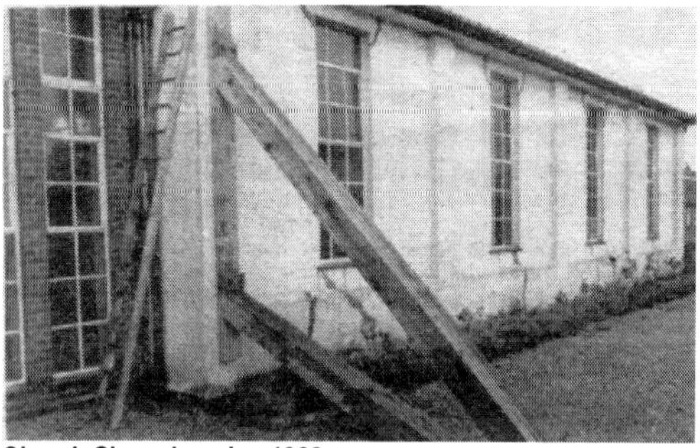

Church Shored-up Jan 1982

The work already carried out had been expensive enough and Fr. Chapman warned the congregation that *'A serious situation faces the church … and that they would be in debt for years to come'*. The projected cost of remedial work was potentially double the cost of building the church! Prayer alone would not be enough to resolve this problem, and permission was finally given to use parish savings towards the total, but they would still have to borrow money for the balance. It was also suggested that parishioners should be encouraged to use Covenants to reclaim tax. With permission and a revised schedule of work obtained, Pynfords were able to give a starting date – November 30th - but the work would make the church unusable. It was now that the practical benefits of good relations developed through Christian Unity and the Council of Churches paid dividends. The Anglican authorities offered the use of the Abbey Church to worship in for as long as they needed it. A very grateful Parish Priest and Catholic Community took up their kind offer and initially planned to be there for only three weeks. Their false optimism turned into two months, and because the Abbey could not accommodate their own services and the Catholics on that 'Special Day', Our Lord's Birth had to be celebrated in its own battered building. Ecumenism had advanced beyond measure, but joint celebration was not on the cards. Fortunately, the first two phases of the underpinning had substantially improved the stability of the building to make it safe enough to inhabit temporarily. And then there was the matter of the mess! A team of parishioners led by Jack Bayles did a splendid job of making the space clean enough to celebrate Christmas Masses; and young people from the Youth Opportunities Scheme were engaged to assist in the final clean-up of the church after the Sanctuary floor had been made good. At last, on 7th February 1982 the Catholic's sojourn as guests in a heritage church came to an end and the community rejoiced in their Lord's House where the Sacred Host was once again reserved in its Tabernacle. How to show gratitude for their kindness and facilitation was no easy matter, so 2 new chairs were donated to The Abbey's own renovation scheme.

Although the church was clean enough after the underpinning work, it looked shabby and needed redecoration. To reduce costs, parishioners were asked to form a taskforce under the guidance of Messrs Daws, Hawkins and Bayles and *'bring their own paintbrush or roller'* to get the job done. Work started on 31st October. In a week, the porch and altar servers Sacristy had been prepared and painted, and two weeks later the ceiling was completed and the work-tower removed, leaving just the lower level work to be finished off.

A sub-committee of the Parish Council was formed to focus and coordinate fund-raising again to pay off this new debt. Halfway through the work, in January 1982, the press suddenly became interested in this local church which might fall down and Fr Chapman was encouraged to give a radio and press interview to raise awareness of the church's plight, which, helpfully, prompted some donations. But the drip-feed of small amounts needed to turn into a heavy trickle. A legacy helped, and by the end of March 1982, 100 members had signed-up to a new Building Fund Lottery in time for its first monthly draw in April which proved effective.

Some small respite was afforded to Fr. Chapman when the Bishop agreed that Fr. Reffitt of Swaffham could take over the responsibility for RAF Watton after the Bishop's visitation on 17th October. Although this left him with the town of Watton to cover, and the job of preaching at the Church Unity Service, it relieved him of the tiring drive on rural roads.

This greatest of misfortunes ironically gave Fr. Chapman a unique legacy: he was the only Catholic Priest since the Reformation to say Mass regularly in the town's former Catholic edifice. The succession of severe problems escalating upon each other left a daunting level of fiscal worry. However, between times, the parish ran smoothly enough with all the aspects associated with a flourishing church taking place. He was well supported too by his parishioners in the practicalities of fund-raising during a very difficult period. In spiritual terms many of Fr. Brophy's ecumenical and inter-faith activities continued to grow, and new Bible Society and study groups started in Wymondham and Hethersett. Liturgically he developed the laity's ministry as Ministers of the Eucharist, and he allowed the folk style music liturgy to be encouraged which now regularly accompanies the whole Mass on a monthly basis to the present day. That Christmas his offertory was the largest he had ever received - £313.

Fr. Joe Farrell, the former Watton parishioner, was finally ordained on 10th July 1982 and until he took up his post as assistant at Bury St Edmunds, on return to the diocese, he provided holiday 'supply' in various parishes. Naturally Fr. Chapman was delighted to have him cover his holiday in early August. Six months later the Bishop sent Fr. Joe back as a locum Parish Priest to tend a bereaved parish when Fr. Chapman died peacefully in the Presbytery on 17th February 1983.

Although his appointment was temporary, as a recently ordained priest he noted some incorrect practises amongst the Faithful and they were pointed out in one of his first bulletins, with liturgical explanation. At the same time the Bishop directed that RAF Watton should once more become Wymondham's responsibility from Easter Sunday, (3rd April). With Watton to cover, Fr. Joe needed more time between

Masses on Sunday to get there. So from Whitsun (22nd May) Mass time was changed by 15 minutes to 09:15. It was helpful too to be able to balance a 'brickbat with a bouquet': the new fund-raising Lottery, started in April the previous year, had raised £1555 – allowing £600 of the debt to be repaid. But even the newest priest found it necessary to remind the Faithful that income was not keeping pace with running costs; and because of financial stringency in the Presbytery, Fr. Joe asked for volunteers on 12th June 1983 to: feed him on Sundays; type up the Bulletin and Rotas for various elements of Sunday church activity; do his and church laundry, and take over the gardening.

With part of his 'apprenticeship' served the Bishop directed him to St Lawrence's Cambridge to complete it. He left on a high note too, when he was able to say that the Building Appeal Fund Lottery, donations and other fund-raising had enabled another £1250 to be sent to the Diocesan Treasurer to offset the huge debt. Thus far, a total of £5000 had been wiped off the debt since 1981. His task had not been to institute change, but he had seen spiritual and social growth come out of bereavement whilst in *locum parentis*. Having originated from Watton he developed a better social environment and connection with that part of the parish. Liturgically he had started House Masses around the community, and enabled the laity as Special Ministers of the Eucharist. As Wymondham waited to welcome Fr. Anthony Foreman from Sudbury, the Bishop rearranged the clergy moves at the last minute and sent someone else instead.

Regrowth and Restructuring

With the parish and its church stabilised Wymondham's next Parish Priest, Fr. Peter Brown, arrived midweek on 21st September 1983. Change was afoot. On his first Sunday Mass parishioners were asked to place a Host on the Paten on entering the church, and a communion offertory procession of the Gifts was instated in the Mass. But the minor illness he brought with him from Downham Market was more than 'flu', and within the week was bed-bound and unable to say Mass. Fr. Chapman's foresight in training some laity as Special Ministers of the Eucharist had proved timely. The situation for which they were needed had occurred; and Eucharistic Services were held on weekdays with Sunday Masses covered by a priest from St George's, Norwich. In this Parish the ministry had proved invaluable, and in September 1984 its uptake was further endorsed by the Bishop. Sixteen people started training in February 1985, and were commissioned on 24th March by Mgr. Harry Wace.

Financial stringency was still necessary and weekday Mass was said in the Presbytery to save heating the church. And it was 30th October before he was recovered enough to say weekday and Sunday Mass. He had also been unimpressed by the Sunday singing and embarked on changes to the music liturgy. In invoking the epithet of St Augustine's that 'he who sings prays twice over', mini practice singing sessions were held and more hymns introduced into the Mass and shorter homilies! A new hymn book finally arrived on November 30th in time for Christmas 1986.

Papal Honours are dispensed infrequently and Peter Hindley was the recipient of the Benemerenti medal for his loyal service within the church, when he retired as organist after 40 years in 1988. Alan Cousin's brief contribution was cut short by an untimely illness and caused Dr Tony Press to take over in 1994. In that same year, the Miller Organ was given to a local rural church when a new electronic organ was donated by Mrs Peggy Murray, in memory of her husband Jack, a former FEPOW. A few years later Roger Noble joined forces with Tony and between them have developed and extended the musical liturgy to the much admired status it enjoys today.

Also on 1st April 1984 Fr. Brown suggested that children from 0-7 years might be usefully engaged and organised as a 'Junior Church' group within the morning Mass leaving after the welcome and returning at the offertory. Fr. Brown was obviously fully recovered from his illness and later that month was, belatedly, officially welcomed to the Parish. His biggest concern now was the poor condition of the Hall, as it would be certain to feature in the 5 yearly Diocesan Surveyor's report. However much a social and fund-raising asset it was, by 1985 the Bishop had made it clear that its replacement would be a long time coming. So the parish community tidied it up with some new curtains, a lick of paint (as and when necessary), and made the best of it.

The excessive cost of heating the church was directly related to old, inefficient electric storage heaters: they had to go! In their place came a modern gas fired system of hot water radiators installed at a cost of £15,000 and functional by October 20th 1984. It was hoped that the church would not only be energy efficient but more comfortable and inviting. To complete his first year the Christmas Bazaar made an enormous profit of £1062 to offset the debt. Next on the list of improvements was to repaint the church outside and update the windows. In early May 1985, the YTS (Youth Training Scheme) were engaged to do the painting, including the Presbytery and the Hall for good measure; followed by double glazed UPVC windows to replace the original Crittall metal casement windows in the church. To increase the capacity custom made, polished wood benches costing £6900 came from Ireland to replace original wooden chairs. Resourceful as ever, some chairs and pews were sold off and monies went towards Parish funds. The icing on the 'comfort cake' was to insulate the church floor with heavy duty carpet from wall to wall including the Sanctuary. And to top it all, the church grounds were landscaped by the Community Service, too, at very little cost. Overall it was a huge outlay, but it looked and felt marvellous: so it was a bonus that in the September the 'Lottery' presented Fr. Peter with another £500 and the Christmas Bazaar made over £1000 again.

Decisions from Vatican II were still coming through and the latest Code of Canon Law was published on 4th December 1983, and more liturgical changes followed. One of the most significant changes was the eventual direction from Maundy Thursday 1986 onwards that receiving Holy Communion under Both Kinds should be standard practice at all Masses

Mass attendance in the parish hovered around 200; but in his 'Christmas Special' Bulletin, Fr. Brown made the point that only 37 parishioners had taken advantage of donating through Tax Covenanting. Although poorly taken up in Fr. Chapman's time, in 1983 the Parish encouragingly received the sum of £1034 from it.

The Catholic Schools in Norwich had long been dependent on Catholic parents from a wider catchment area to send their children to their three schools to maintain numbers. Concerned to do 'their bit', several Wymondham Catholic parents, and parishioners, formed a School Bus Committee in 1979. They hired a private coach to transport children to the First and Middle Schools helped by travel subsidies for Voluntary Aided School-children from Norfolk County Council. On safety grounds, the local coach firm, Semmence, required an adult to 'ride shotgun' and be responsible for them, and so a rota of parents was organised. But as subsidies were reduced, the cost to individual families increased and as numbers dwindled, creative ways of fund-raising were devised by the committee to subsidise the cost and eke out its existence. Before the summer holidays, pleas were again voiced by the committee for local Catholics to send their children to the Catholic Schools in Norwich. By Sept 21st 1990, when the Diocesan Schools levy doubled from £1400 to £2852, Wymondham Catholic children occupied 6% of places in these schools.

Further out in the community there was some difficulty again at RAF Watton. In January 1979 Fr. Chapman couldn't get in to say Mass because the RAF had 'lost' the keys to the Station Church. Five years hence the difficulty getting access was security related due to IRA activity. The station Church was closed on July 25th 1993, and the RAF made the old Officers Mess dining room into a chapel which Catholics used until it finally closed down and was sold for housing development.

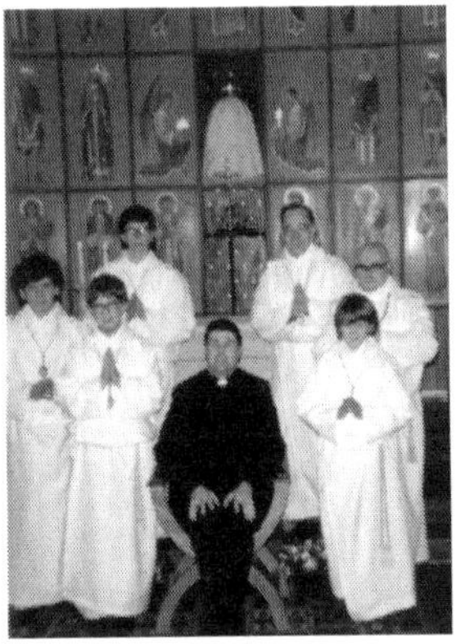

1985: New Albs for Servers
S.Head; A.Donnelly; J.Lang (MC); J.Budgen (MC); D.Pell; Fr. Brown; N.Lysons

Some thirty or so years earlier, Fr. Cowin had set-up the Altar Servers Guild and equipped the boys with cassocks and cottas. However, by this time not only was the style dated, but replacements were necessary. In response to an appeal for monies to make them 'in-house', two enterprising parishioners embarked on a 'Sponsored Slim' to buy the fabric. By Christmas 1985 Mrs Jenny Lysons had made and kitted out all the Altar Servers with much admired lightweight, modern albs and cinctures, and with some other additions and replacements, the style remains in use today (2012).

The male only preserve ended in April 1994 when permission to admit females to the Altar Server's Guild was granted. The PP offered the opportunity soon afterwards and it was quickly taken up by Claire Wiseman and Claire Engler; the first girls to serve Our Lord at the Altar. Pictured also is

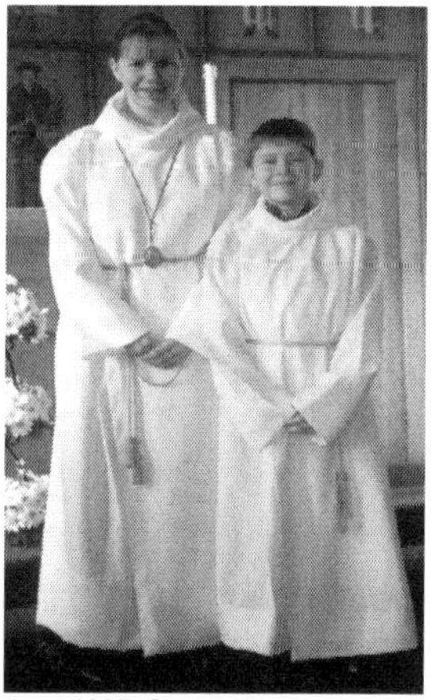

June 1995: Claire Wiseman Trailblazer - & newest server Michael Wiseman Age 7

the Altar boy who became Wymondham's first recipient of the Guild's Silver Medal in 2007, serving continuously from the Sunday after his First Holy Communion for 12 years, a feat which has not yet been equalled.

The seed of social and spiritual inclusion recently sown by Fr. Farrel through House Masses in Watton had little time to become effective, and were restarted by Fr. Brown in June 1984: Attleborough and Tacolneston at first with more following in other outlying areas. To promote this exercise widely, a Parish Picnic was proposed to be held close to the church's Saint's Patronal feast day. The Parish took to this with great enthusiasm, and with their Parish Priest in his element and out of his 'Sunday Best', they indulged and socialised in the grounds of a parishioner's large house with a swimming pool in Tacolneston. People brought their own picnic so there was no cost – just fun. A few years later the successful annual event moved to the extensive grounds of Eccles Hall School. The popular event continues, albeit in slightly different format and venue, today. More social (and fund-raising) events followed, each little profit raised steadily chipping away at the debt. An idea that came out of this get-together was a Parish Directory to use as a quick reference guide for contacts in the Parish and hopefully reduce calls to the PP for just a telephone number etc. In the November of 1984, his parish boundaries were changed and Mulbarton came into the fold of this shepherd, just as the Parish Directory was available.

With so much going on within an enlarged Parish, 1986 saw Fr. Peter getting some assistance. First to arrive was Fr. Tim

Wright OSB on loan to the Parish for a year to help out at weekends, and turning up on his 750cc Twin motorbike, gave new meaning to 'The Rev Father' and a certain 'street cred' with the youngsters A fortnight later, an American Nun Sr. Alies Thérèse of Peace (a consecrated solitary), was appointed by the Bishop as a Pastoral Assistant working mainly in Attleborough in an enabling ministry. A special Mass in the presence of the Bishop was arranged 30th March for her to take her final vows in Wymondham.

Reaching out into the community, the church extended a welcome to the local Brownies and Guides to attend a church Parade on December 2nd 1984. The hoped for benefit of the church feeling a welcoming space to be in had been achieved and Mass numbers were regularly above 250 too.

Several years previously the Stable Youth Club had folded and once again the young people needed an outlet for their energy. A series of mini-Discos were organised for both 7-10s and 11-16 year old children from October 27th. This became a regular feature on the first Saturday of the month. The young people were also determined to play their part towards paying off the church's debt and they presented Fr. Brown with a cheque from its profits in June 1986. The Youth Day planned for July 6th 1986 also went ahead with the Brownies attending again. Attendance varied but gradually less of the church's own youngsters were using it. Local gate-crashers finally put paid to it in April 1987 when, regrettably, they caused trouble in the discos and outside the Hall with the result that, sadly, the discos were discontinued in May.

Parish boundaries were redrawn again, and Fr. Brown's patch grew to accommodate the Carmelite Convent at Quidenham, Eccles and Wilby from December 14th 1986. After Christmas the Vicar General added East Harling and Harling Road for good measure. It was complete when technical jurisdiction followed in October 1987, with responsibility for The Meltons, Wramplingham and Carleton Forehoe. However, in practise the latter additions did not actively affect Wymondham's numbers, as people there were closer to the Cathedral, and were unlikely to change allegiance.

Britain's wonderful weather reared an ugly head again in the winter of 1986, but with the heating kept on day and night to prevent frozen pipes, the new central heating system proved its worth, even if at a cost. Pleas were made to keep up regular giving even if prevented from getting to Mass. Later that year the now infamous hurricane storm of October 1987 fortunately caused little damage to Church property: the new roof survived with loss of a ridge tile and the Presbytery had a single slate down; but the lean-to carport attached to the house blew away again and the boundary fence was a casualty needing major repair. But the skills were in the parish, and to save money, a working party of parishioners repaired it on November 15th.

The Diocesan consultation document put out for the laity to consider in October 1986 resulted in a refocusing of Parish Councils remits. In Wymondham its former role was extended to assist the Parish Priest as: the Parish Pastoral Council to help with general parochial concerns, and a Finance Committee created. Their first meeting was 2nd July 1987. The cohesive effect of house masses helped to develop the outlying communities and drew in the most recent villages added to the Parish. Each community was represented and encouraged to voice their concerns and ideas. One concern was the need for a ramp at the church door and Mr Peter Mahoney volunteered to oversee its construction.

The young people decided that they wanted a children's bulletin, and a group led by Justine Dowsing and Kathleen Head arranged with Fr. Peter to produce it for Christmas 1987 on December 20th. The exercise was repeated on Easter Sunday.

Sr. Alies Thérèse ministry with the young people of the Parish, produced an outstanding display at the Diocesan Assembly in 1987, and brought them together in 1988 to work on, and produce a modern Passion Play for Holy Week enacted in the church by the confirmation group of that year, which was an enormous success.

Spirit of Christmas. . . .

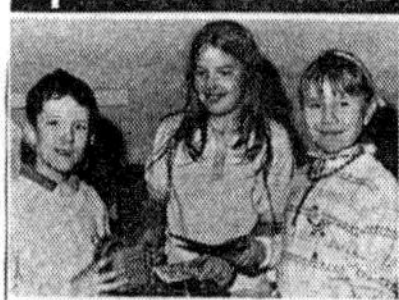

A Christmas bazaar in Wymondham raised over £2,000 at the weekend.

Organised by a committee of Catholics from all parts of the parish — as far afield as Quidenham and Watton — it was hailed as a great success and the money will be used for general developments within the parish.

Several hundred people passed through the doors of the Central Hall on Saturday.

"It was a great success. People have been planning it for about 11 months," said Father Peter Brown.

• Preparing goodies for the lucky dip are (from left): David Bates, Margaret Pell and Clare Wiseman.

. . . at Wymondham Catholic bazaar

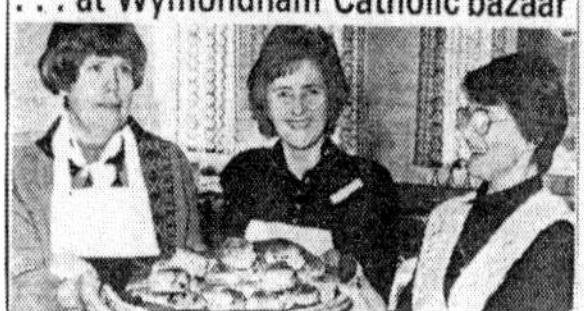

• Tea ladies (from left): Teresa Balls, Thelma Carter and Joan Barry.

We can't let the Christmas Fayre pass by without some very special thanks to all who organised, gave, bought and helped in any way.
Some people were working away for <u>months</u> beforehand and had their homes and personal lives considerably inconvenienced with storing and pricing of goods.
Others have been busy with needles etc. for months.
Thank you all.
The next planning meeting for November 25th 1989 !!! will be on Thursday 20th April after evening Mass.

Evangelism call by bishop to his flock

THE Roman Catholic Bishop of East Anglia urges his flock to become evangelists in a new blueprint for the church in the region just published.

Bishop Alan Clark makes the call to urge Catholics to take their message to everyone in and out of the church community in a new five-year pastoral plan for the diocese called "Deepening and Widening Our Faith".

The bishop writes in the hardback book: "The secularisation of the modern world at home and abroad now requires of Christians a positive commitment to living and teaching the values of the Gospel."

In calling for pastoral councils to be formed in all parishes and for working parties to study and report on key issues, including lay ministry and evangelisation, he stressed: "We are in the business of evangelisation on all fronts, inside and outside the Church.

"If we are asked what our resource is, the answer is clear. Our resource is you — not alone but together."

Already, the 160-strong diocesan pastoral council has been appointed to implement the pastoral plan which it is hoped to fulfill in five years.

A Pastoral Development Fund is to be set up with the aim of raising £100,000 to pay for the work.

There are 80,000 Roman Catholics in Norfolk, Suffolk and Cambridgeshire and it is estimated that number will grow by 30,000 in the next 10 years.

"We are a small but fast-growing diocese," said diocesan communications officer Rev Gary Dowsey.

The above appeared in the "E.D.P." last Monday. It shows how much interest there is in this book which is the official Pastoral Plan for our Diocese for the next five years.
We have 30 copies of the book in the parish - one for every ten Mass-goers. However, if there is a demand we can obtain further copies. If the copies in YOUR part of the parish are all gone, please 'phone Father Brown who will obtain some more to satisfy the needs.
The book is very reasonably priced at £2.

With a number of ethnic immigrants arriving in the surrounding area, she also set up the East Anglian Racial Awareness Project, which was aimed at just that, and the outward looking community supported it for many years.

1989 saw the church take advantage of another modern phenomenon, the Car Boot Sale. Its large car-park fronting onto a main thoroughfare into the town was ideally placed to catch passers-by. At £5 per 'boot spot' these events became quite popular and an effective fund-raiser. Eventually they evolved to Table top sales in the Hall. Unfortunately it was the year that the church was robbed too, when the keys were lost and money stolen from the safe.

In Fr. Cowin's time he said Mass every day for deceased FEPOW and turned a page of the Books of Remembrance; but since the new church was opened to great rejoicing, , FEPOW had not congregated here as a memorial body. It was in 1989 that the KSC asked for a Foundation Mass to the memory of FEPOW. The Norwich Fellowship of FEPOW was contacted to join in its celebration, but they had been holding their own services in in Norwich since 1946 and were not aware of the Catholic Memorial Church ten miles down the road. Three years later they were eventually persuaded by Peter Wiseman to come to an evening ecumenical service in 1992 on 14th May (The Relief of Rangoon). Thanks to ecumenism they came and left, feeling encouraged that the memory of their fallen comrades was important and hallowed. They have returned every year since though fewer in number due to infirmity.

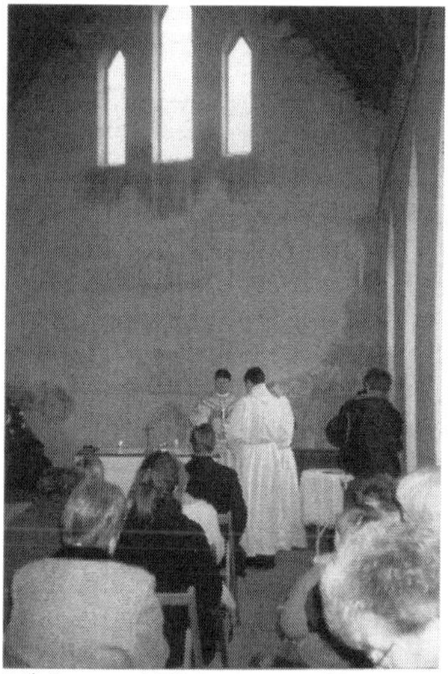

14th January 1992 Anniversary Mass
Priest: Fr Brown; MC John Budgen
Altar Server James Dunne

1992 was a special year, as several Anniversaries occurred, not least the 40th Anniversary of the church opening and more importantly 80th Anniversary of the first Catholic service in Wymondham. A year of celebrations was held, with a Mass taking place in Cock Street Chapel Building, by kind permission of Mr & Mrs Wood, (then owners) and subsequently a celebration event happened every month. And the Bishop celebrated the Ruby Anniversary Mass in the church that a Catholic Priest's vow had built 40 years ago.

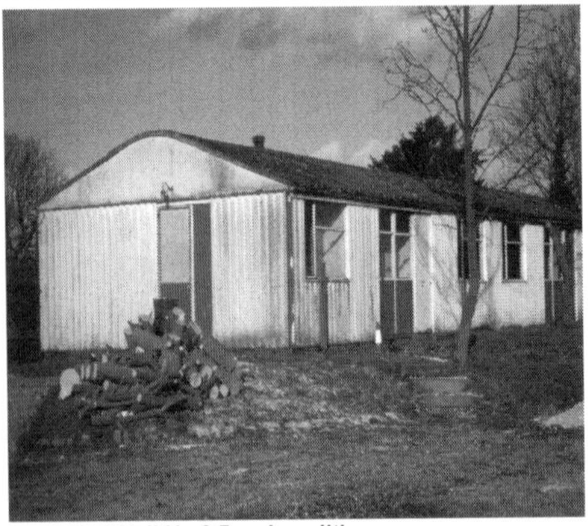
April 1995 Hall No.2 Pre-demolition
(Logs are remains of Apple Trees)

Several bequests had been made specifically designated towards a new Hall, and fund-raising was on-going to clear the debt. But deteriorating buildings seem to attract trouble, and in February 1994 the Hall was vandalised and a new lock had to be fitted. Money was in the pot waiting for permission to be given for what everyone knew was needed. That day arrived on Bishop Clark's retirement in April 1994 when one of his last decisions was to give Wymondham the go ahead to build the hall. With plans in place, a Musical farewell entertainment was held on 4th December 1994, and the Local Planning Authority gave their consent on February 1st, 1995. Demolition soon began and the site cleared, taking away the last apple trees of the orchard where Fr. Phillips had said his Office 70 years earlier. Building was completed by the summer and the footprint of the new building was half as big as the original with separate commercial style catering facilities and upgraded toilet facilities.

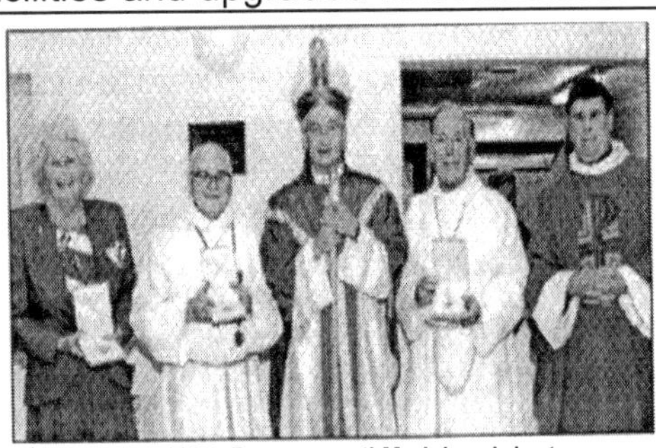
3rd November 1995: Benemerenti Medal recipients

After his installation in January 1995 as 2nd Bishop of East Anglia, Peter Smith's first official visitation to Wymondham on 3rd November 1995 was initially to confer the Sacrament of Confirmation. But there were three agendas: One known, one obvious, and one secret! The obvious one was to officially open and Bless the hall; but unbeknown to the parish, and the recipients, the Papal Honour of the Benemerenti Medal was to be presented to three parishioners for their outstanding devotion to the church and church work over 60 years. They were: John and Irene Lang and John Budgen. A real triumph of Catholic Christian service in Wymondham, that had seen four of its parishioners honoured by the Pope within seven years.

After the unedifying religious bigotry experienced by some Catholics in the second decade of the twentieth century, ecumenical efforts had encouraged Wymondham's Catholic Parish to be able to exhibit its early history through one of the inaugural displays in the new Heritage Museum in the Bridewell, on the corner opposite the church between May and September 1996.

By the time Fr. Peter finally gave over the Parish to 'younger blood' in August 1997, his 'patch' covered over 300 square miles, and he had celebrated his Silver Jubilee as a Priest. He was transferred to Cromer and left a legacy of some note, with its new Parish Hall being one of his achievements. While his incumbency of 14 years fell short of Fr. Cowin's span, the 'Living Memorial' had been transformed into a warmer, more inviting space where all were welcomed in relative comfort. The Parish had been restructured around its communities, and like a wheel, outlying parts of the parish were more spiritually connected with Wymondham at the centre as its hub. Parish administration had been restructured with updated remits reflecting current situations of the church and society. Security had been improved too. The ecumenical efforts of Fr. Brophy had continued to grow and develop with its Catholic Community deepening and widening their Faith through the Council of Churches, Christian Aid, Church Unity, and reaching out to youth organisations locally and in the Diocese. He was given the important job of Chancellor of the Diocese in January 1995. And six months before he left welcomed Fr. George Bennett to assist him in the parish from March 1997.

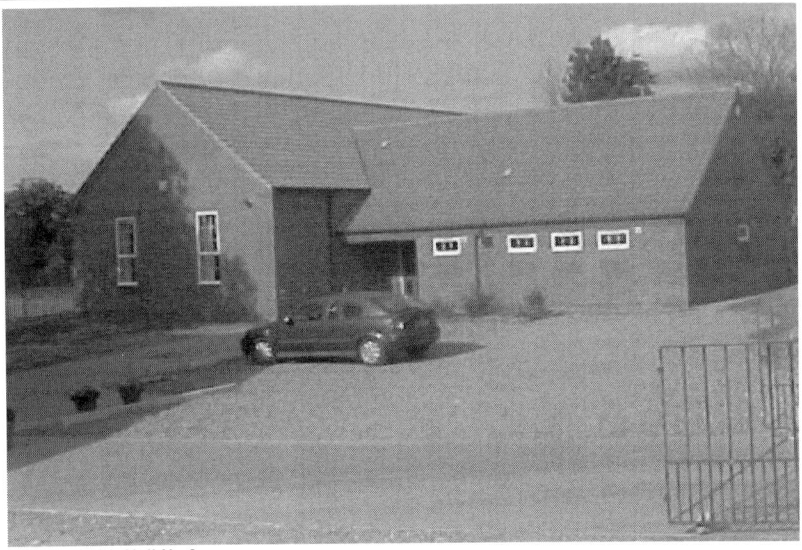

October 2001: Hall No.3

Development and Extension

Fr. David Jennings, one of East Anglia's ordinands in 1993, moved from inner-city Cambridge to take his place as PP of rural Wymondham in September 1997. The Parish was still large, its congregation still growing, and Mass times remained the same. Now that Fr. George Bennet was here to assist, care of Attleborough's Catholics was returned to Wymondham's PP, while Fr. Roger Spencer retained spiritual care of the Carmelite Convent at Quidenham. And there were plans ... more changes!

Earlier reordering of the Sanctuary had left the Altar only two levels above the body of the church, and to adhere to liturgical norms an additional step was needed; and as the Eternal Flame was now suspended from the south Sanctuary wall, a symbolic dove took its place directly over the Altar. Other liturgically correct repositioning of statues took place after the Memorial Chapel was refurbished, and an appropriate stand purchased for the Processional Cross. Without a designated baptistery area, the font had been found a space in front of the Sanctuary. A custom made Holy Oils Aumbry, to house the Oils consecrated at the Chrism Mass, was given in 1998 and positioned above the font in full view of the Faithful.

The introduction of the Ministry of Welcome in March 1998 extended the role of the laity as the first point of contact on entering the church, and has continued to date. Changing social pressures and lifestyles were issues to which the Church needed to respond. Within the year it was clear to Fr. David that attendance at Saturday's anticipatory Mass in Hethersett, (and Mass at RAF Watton) were diminishing, and after consultation, Holyday Mass was transferred to the nearest Sunday at Wymondham from October 3rd. Similarly, later in October the frequency of House Masses changed from monthly to quarterly.

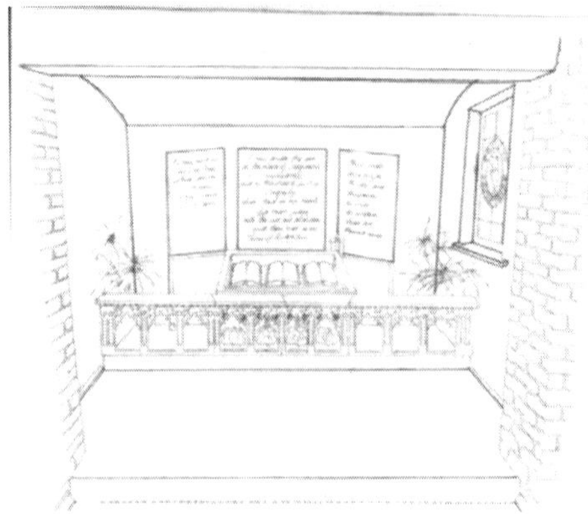

Sketch of Proposed FEPOW Memorial Chapel

The planned Memorial Chapel in the church's original design did not get built, and 45 years later, the Lady Chapel's original purpose had been overtaken. A pragmatic solution was to turn this former devotional space into the Memorial Chapel that Fr. Cowin had wanted, with the Books of Remembrance enshrined within. A fund started on August 30th 1998 to refurbish it and recreate it as a fitting shrine. The FEPOW Committee set up in September agreed that a stained glass FEPOW emblem would be included, and the carved Oak Altar Rail that had been cut down was restored to fit inside the side-chapel when refurbishment work started on May 30th 1999. Fr. David now turned his attention to extending the existing church as Mass attendance was still increasing as a result of housing developments locally.

So in December 1998, the Diocesan Surveyor was asked to undertake a feasibility study to develop the porch area of the church. The cleared area behind the Presbytery, formerly housing the stable church, was now a valuable asset. As planning permission was granted on 9th May 1999 the Diocesan Land Agent could put it up for sale. It sold! The inaugural meeting of the Porch Development Project Group took place on 20th August 1999 followed by a small exhibition of proposed plans on September 12th. It was planned as a Jubilee Project for the 3rd Millennium and by October 3rd the Parish had raised the encouraging sum £10,000 and by the time planning permission had been given the Jubilee account stood at £85,000.

This leap in the total was partly achieved in an unusual way: on February 6th 2000, Fr. David challenged parishioners to emulate the Parable of The Talents in St. Luke's Gospel (Luke: 19)! The 'Talent' was £10, which he gave to anyone who took up the challenge to increase it and return the sums achieved to the Jubilee Fund. One hundred and eighteen people took part and a diverse range of talents were employed in increasing the Talent: jam making; cake baking; baby-sitting; car washing and a group of young people created a cookery booklet which they sold, and as far as is known, no-one was 'cast out' for not having increased their Talent. A local supermarket was also persuaded to donate jars of jam to the church, and the priest distributed it to people who were tasked with eating the contents and returning the jar filled with coins.

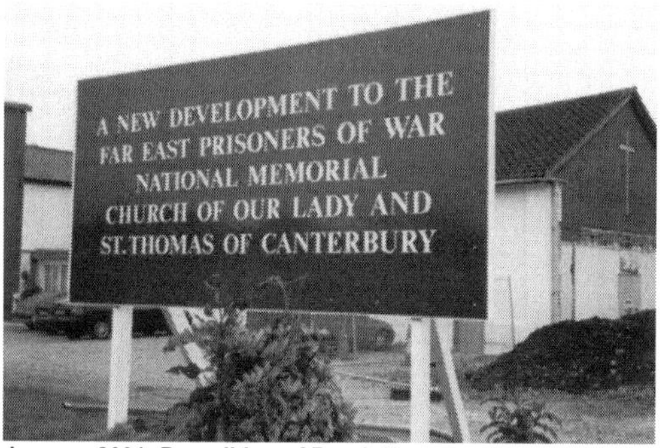

January 2001: Demolition of Porch No.2

.

Work started on 12th March 2001 and was completed on October 15th. Although demolition removed the glass brick Cross in the gable end its illuminated message would survive. The topping-out ceremony was as distinctive as the new Cross was unique. This extra-ordinary Cross was lowered by the PP into a glass panelled section of the ridge directly above the baptismal font. Its unique design ensures that from whichever direction it is viewed, it will still appear as a Cross. More than that, when the Narthex is lit up in the evenings the Cross visibly proclaims that Christ is present here, just as originally intended.

The second extension gave the church more than Porch No.3. It was half the size of the original church and provided a multipurpose room, and necessary supporting facilities in addition to the new Narthex area. The original Font, gifted by the CWL in May 1954 was too small for this welcoming space and a large octagonal Font, rescued from demolition, was installed under an orbital frame of lights. The original wooden altar panels, now conserved, were displayed and lit inside the entrance and two time-capsules, one compiled by the adults and the other by children of the parish, were sealed under the Jubilaeum stone to release their secrets in another century. A carved oak Patronal statue of St Thomas A'Becket was commissioned and situated in a niche in the original wall of the church, and underneath, a small alcove contains FEPOW artefacts from the infamous Burma-Siam Railway. In particular the original Memorial stone indicating the reason for this church's presence was located on the external wall of the entrance.

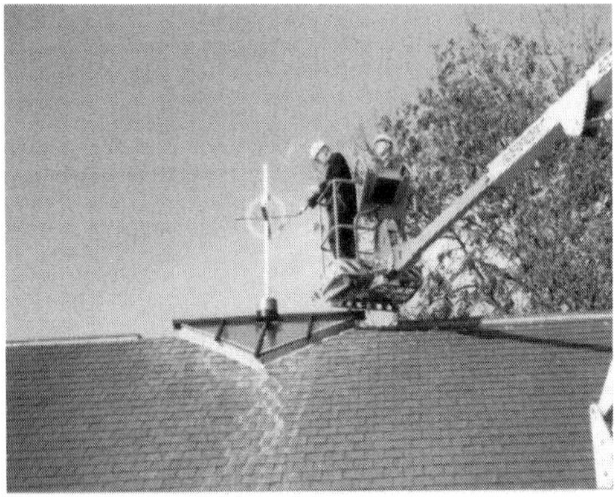

October 2001: Fr Jennings Topping-Out - A unique Cross

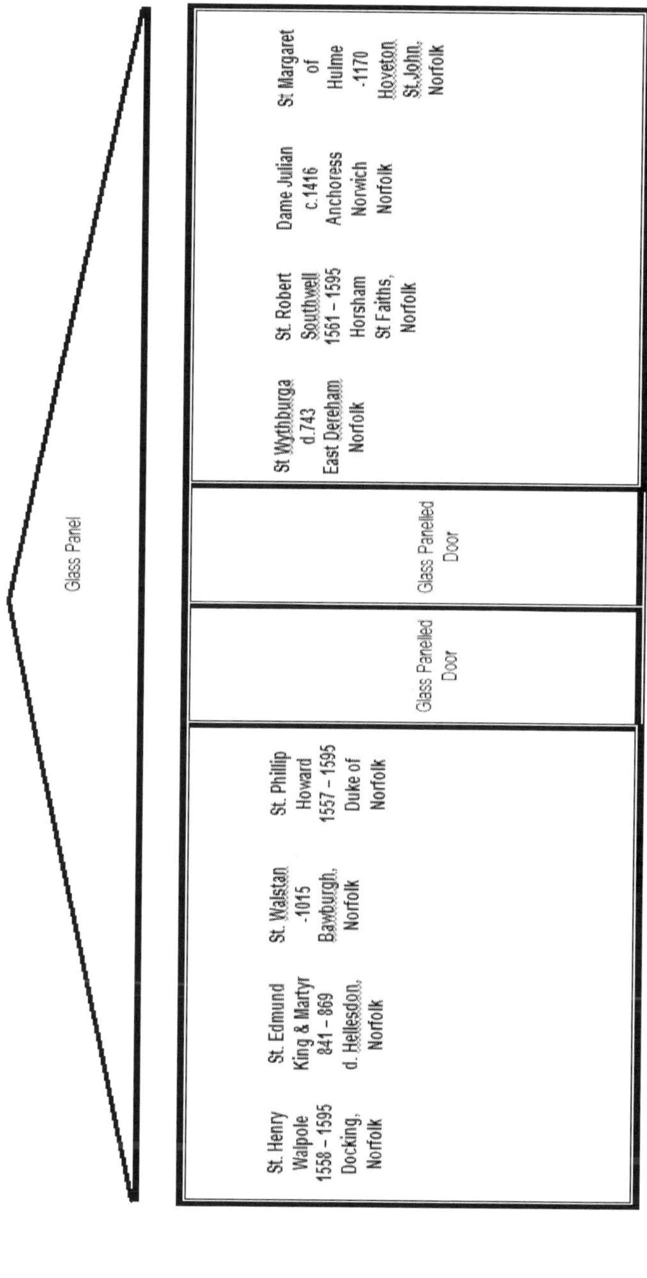

Saints on the Narthex Panels 2001

Hitherto, all previous buildings in which this Community had worshipped had only been blessed when opened; but at last the conditions allowing consecration had been met. 'Everyone' wanted to be at this Mass! But just as admission was by ticket in 1952, Fr. David had to contend with Health and Safety Regulations as well as the 'simple practicalities' that limited numbers and admission by ticket. That year's confirmation candidates were present as the saintly relics were received into the church the day before the ceremony. Finally, on Saturday 27th October 2001, at 11.30am. Bishop Peter Smith conducted the divine process of Consecration and sealed relics of St Thomas of Canterbury, St Gregory, and St Maximillian Kolbe into the Altar. Three months earlier, in July 2001, Fr. George Bennet had gone to his reward, and in March 2002, 12 Consecration Crosses were given in grateful memory of his priestly life and placed around the church.

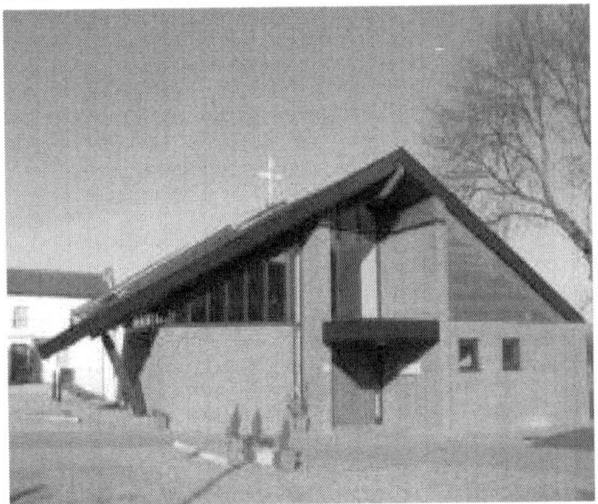

Our Lady & St. Thomas of Canterbury September 2000 (Narthex Extension)

In spiritual terms, the Parish's commitment to catechesis was encapsulated in a prospectus entitled *Enriching Our Faith* in 1998 and on September 12th Bishop Peter Smith had accepted a nomination for the Permanent Diaconate, culminating in his ordination in October 2002. While liturgically, said Mass was developed to a sung Mass with the Master of the Music, Tony Press. Modern Mass settings were used, and a Cantor was introduced to lead the psalm and congregational responses. With recent changes in the Mass new settings are being introduced. Other sacred music events were introduced to the parish with an Easter cantata, *'Jerusalem Joy'* by Roger Jones, undertaken by Roger Noble in 2000 and other cantatas have been performed as a biennial event.

It was suggested that the Parish should prepare for the forthcoming Great Christian Jubilee at the end of 1999. As the schools went back in September Fr. David asked parishioners to set aside the 27th /28th November for a weekend of spiritual renewal under the banner of 'Celebrating Our Faith'. Events included an outside speaker, Fr. Raphael Esteban, several workshops, and community social activities. There would only be one celebration of Mass in the parish that Sunday, and to have the whole parish together required a bigger space: and Wymondham High School was hired for the occasion. As a fitting end to the celebration, everyone gathered on the grass for a communal panoramic photograph.

To celebrate the 3rd Millennium and four decades of ecumenical growth and development in Wymondham, 'Churches Together', the body that replaced the Council of Churches locally, engaged a local artist to create a Millennium Triptych of people from its three main church communities. People from each church involved volunteered to be photographed and their pictures then transferred onto three large canvasses on separate frames, which when completed, were displayed side by side as a triptych. It was then put on show at each of those churches in turn over the year.

There is perhaps no better indication of Catholic integration into the fabric of society than to have its parishioners serve its local community: in March 1993, Bob Buscall of Carbrooke had been elected to Civic office as High Sheriff of Norfolk with Fr. Brown as his Chaplain. More recently, on March 12th 2000, the Civic Service was held in Wymondham's Catholic Church for the first time after Councillor Joe Mooney had been elected Mayor. And in 2001, Fr. David was invited to be the first RC Chaplain of the local British Legion Branch.

Both spiritually and physically, Fr. Jennings had led a thriving Roman Catholic Parish into the 3rd Millennium and met the demands of expanding numbers. The church building had been developed spectacularly, and gained the Norfolk County Council Design Award in 2002 for its distinctive extension. Security of the church's property was significantly upgraded in January 1999 with anti-vandal fencing erected in place of the disintegrating wooden fence with other measures included for the Presbytery. The benefits of ecumenism have enabled the importance of the 'Debt of Honour' to FEPOW to be recognised and their remembrance developed into an ecumenical Memorial service for FEPOW in May each year. With his help, the committee had raised its profile by encouraging senior representatives from Military Attaches to Chelsea Pensioners, FEPOW and local dignitaries to attend a service with an invited speaker and buffet before as well as having a post service reception.

This significant labour came to an end when the Bishop gave him a different challenge in Peterborough, and he left at the end of August 2003.

A Mission Beyond the Parish

After completing his doctorate in Rome and Oxford an author, Fr. Sean Connolly, arrived as Wymondham's next Parish Priest in early September 2003 from his curacy in Great Yarmouth.

Incoming priests always inherit something from their predecessor, and Fr. Sean was no different: one thing was a positive example of Wymondham's Catholics exhibiting care for its community. 'Helping Hands' had been established in January 2003, by a group of Parishioners under the guidance of Fr. Gordon Cordy, and gave practical and spiritual support to the housebound and isolated. He also inherited the task of collating the Parish's responses to Bishop Michael's consultation paper which would form part of the Diocesan Pastoral Plan. This had wider implications than boundary changes and the projected shortfall of priests.

Hitherto, help for the priest in the parish office had only been *ad hoc*, but modern parochial workloads highlighted the benefit of better secretarial support. So it was a great relief when Mrs Maggie Picton took up her post as the first official Parish secretary 2½ days a week until she emigrated to Canada in early 2005.

Forging humanitarian and educational links in developing countries has long been a part of Christian culture. A valuable part of the Norwich Catholic Schools' outreach programme was the educational link with St. Mary's school in Zomba, Malawi, and teacher's exchange visits that flowed from it. While visiting in 2003, two teachers from Zomba were invited to address Wymondham's congregation after Sunday Mass on 4th October to highlight the plight of reduced resources. From their talk, a proactive idea of fostering and developing a parish link with Zomba's Catholic parish of St Charles Lwanga emerged. The unified backing of Priest, PPC and Finance

Committee was enthusiastic, and the Parish, a one-time Poor Mission, had no qualms about supporting a Malawi Project. Groups and individuals were encouraged to send a wide and informative profile of the Parish. From regular communications, Fr. Sean had picked up that there was an urgent need to secure the church boundary in the form of wall to prevent illegal building on church land. If not put in place, any subsequent project could not be considered. Fund-raising ensued and the parish's generosity knew no bounds, raising £2000 in a short period of time enabling them to make the bricks and construct the wall. In the following February (2005), a parish delegation with educational and clerical backgrounds, four ladies and a Deacon, embarked on a visit to St Charles Lwanga Parish to establish and develop personal contacts. The only stipulation being that they should be self-funding and feedback findings to the Parish. On their return, the Malawi Steering Group was formed to coordinate fund-raising and liaison with Zomba. After much consultation with much consultation with and between parishes, they decided that a Maize Mill would be the most useful item from their 'wish list' of possible projects. Wymondham agreed that it was fiscally practical to do within a 5 year timeframe. But reaching outside the Parish was not that simple a task and fund-raising the least of its difficulties as it did not come to fruition until another Parish Priest was at the helm.

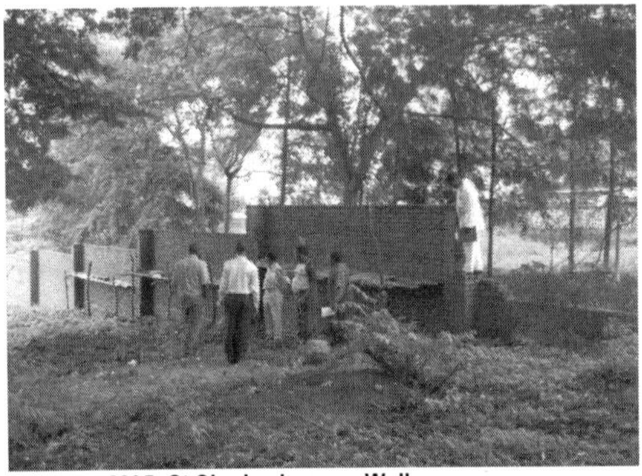

February 2005: St Charles Lwanga Wall

During Church Unity Week in January 2004 decades of ecumenical effort between the churches in Wymondham paid dividends for Fr. Sean in terms of the support and welcome given by fellow ministers of other traditions. Lenten lunches this year took place in a different church each week and the Women's World Day of Prayer, an established link developed several years previously, now rotated annually to a different church with the Catholics hosting it in February 2005.

'Away-day' Parish Retreats to Clare Priory and Hermitage Hall were arranged at the end of June 2004 and Fr. Sean encouraged those involved in any of the ministries to go. After the Summer Hog Roast – the successor to the Parish Picnic event - in July, early August 2004 saw the first introduction of a Parish Renewal Course. The 'CaFÉ evangelistic video presentations were a series of evening meetings hosted by different volunteer groups in the church and led by Fr. Sean. The thought provoking spiritual topics and issues proved most popular, attracting between 70 and 95 people to each event over the seven weeks it was on.

The Books of Remembrance have been the source of enquiry since 1957 and as requests became more frequent it was necessary to make names easier to locate. Computer technology made this possible and an electronic database the ideal solution. Although one had been started it was unwieldy, and Brian Holloway from Hingham created a usable database. By 1998 a website was desirable and Neil Mahoney was asked to create the first FEPOW website before he moved away. Technology improved dramatically and Ian Lester and his son Jonathan, an IT professional overhauled the database and revamped the FEPOW website re-launching it in April 2005. Two years later a Parish website was launched on the internet and Ian managed the insertion of FEPOW names into the database. Enquiries can be addressed more easily and personal visits of relatives quickly arranged.

Fr. Sean had packed quite a lot into his short time, but Our Lord had other plans for him and he was granted a sabbatical to further his studies in July 2005. His legacy was one of looking outwards to Africa, a modern focus on spiritual renewal and vocational insights in a technological age. The Parish was sorry to see him go, but very grateful that Fr. Brendan Moffat came to tide the parish over until the next incumbent took up residence.

Time For Consolidation

Another Ex-Army Chaplain, Fr. Dick White, was 'posted in' as Wymondham's next incumbent on September 18th 2005. He was inducted by Bishop Michael Evans on October 7th and would celebrate the 20th anniversary of his Ordination in July 2010.

Inheriting a strong and committed community of Faith poses challenges that differ from those faced by early Mission Priests, but the structures in place allowed Fr. Dick to enhance them in his own way. The aim may still be the same, but the task was different: one of consolidating the collective efforts of nine decades of development, and in 2012, preparing for the unknown.

Fr. Dick arrived just as the parish were preparing for the fund-raising Autumn Fair on October 16th. Zomba's Maize Mill was an inherited project to which the Parish was committed, and the Malawi Steering Group had recently announced that £5,000 needed to be raised. However, Malawi's cultural differences, planning processes and land purchase significantly delayed completion of the project in the anticipated timescale. In the meantime St Charles Lwanga's Parish Priest made a reciprocal visit in June 2006 and their new Parish Priest,

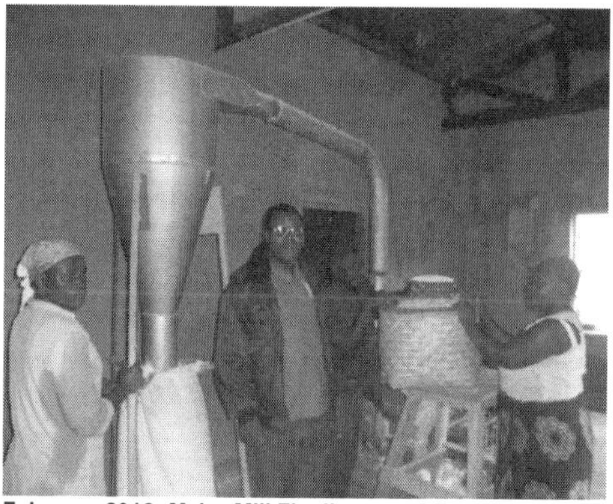

February 2012: Maize Mill Finally up and Running
Fr. Ignacio Bokosi

Fr. Ignacio Bokosi, accompanied by two members of his parish, en route to a conference in England, visited Wymondham the following May.

During the 2005 visit to Malawi, their parishioners had expressed disappointment that no young people were in the group. On the occasion of St. Charles Lwanga Parish 40th Anniversary celebrations, Paul Robertson, a young person, travelled to visit them as a representative from Wymondham Parish on July 13th 2008 and on his return Paul gave a short presentation to the parish.

By 2009 Fr. Ignacio had left St Charles Lwanga Parish but while in England visited his Friends in Wymondham and informed them that the land for the Maize Mill had finally been purchased. But it was February 2012 before news from Malawi let the Parish know that the Maize Mill was finally up & running.

In November 2005, soon after Fr. Dick's arrival, there was good news from the Finance Committee: the Parish was free of debt for the first time in 5 years. However, the rising cost of living and increasing parish expenses prompted their ever-recurring plea for parishioners to take up tax covenants. The challenges of fund-raising remain and are always different and evolving, but with the cottage behind the Presbytery now refurbished it was providing an income just as the Building Fund Lottery had done for 28 years. But it had been gradually losing its members, despite attempts to revive interest. It had provided a steady trickle of funds to help pay off the Parish debt but it was clear in January 2010 that it had run its course and it closed in March.

Any organisation such as a parish depends on the goodwill of an army of volunteers. Their practical expertise, tolerance and good humour is necessary for its smooth running. This is no more evident than when secretarial support lapsed in 2005. In the interim that vital communication link, The Bulletin, had at times required the PP to demonstrate his typing skills. However a talented a number of volunteers came forward to assist in its production. A permanent solution came when a part-time Parish Administrator was employed in July 2011.

Lenten observance in 2007 introduced a quiet period of prayer and meditation one evening a week in the Meeting Room. In 2008 Wymondham's Catholics had a foretaste of what Parish 'clustering' arrangements might entail as the Lent Reconciliation Service was a joint one with Our Lady & St. Walston's in Costessey.

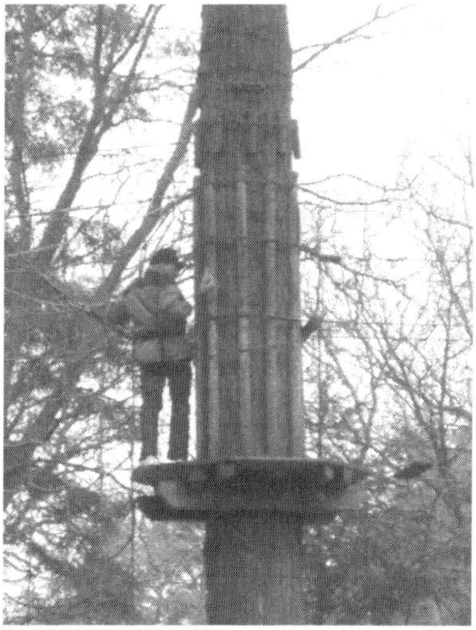
2012: Leap of Faith...

Priests have always encouraged the youth of the church as altar servers to enhance and facilitate the liturgical ceremonies, and Fr. Dick has been no different in that respect; more particularly he has enthusiastically endorsed the late Bishop's vision of involving the young people in other areas of lay ministry which were traditionally the preserve of adults. Wymondham Parish proudly shows that its young people are actively involved as Readers, as Extraordinary Ministers of the Eucharist and in Catechesis.

The step of Faith that is Confirmation is an important transition for young people in the church. Several very engaged and successful groups have been taken through this spiritual development. In the absence of a Bishop the 2012 group had the special honour of being confirmed by their Parish Priest, and as a group they were 'treated' to a team-building away-day at an adventure centre in Thetford Forest where the young people 'swung' through the trees with their priest, catechists and some parents. This symbolic leap of faith has a significance that has echoed in the community over the last century.

Political intrigues at the Town Council in October 2011 thrust the church and diocese unwillingly into the public eye over the proposed commercial development of the historic King's Head Meadow. This grassed area which is a boundary of the church site, was where the first Missioners held their open-air Mass, the first since the Reformation in1911. A century later it, and now the church, were once again placed in the spotlight. Whilst that threat has receded, this community will have to have Faith that it should remain here.

One hundred years of Catholicism is being marked by the erection of a contemporary crucifix above the Sanctuary arch, this book and a parish celebration meal which will coincide with the 60th anniversary of the opening of this church.

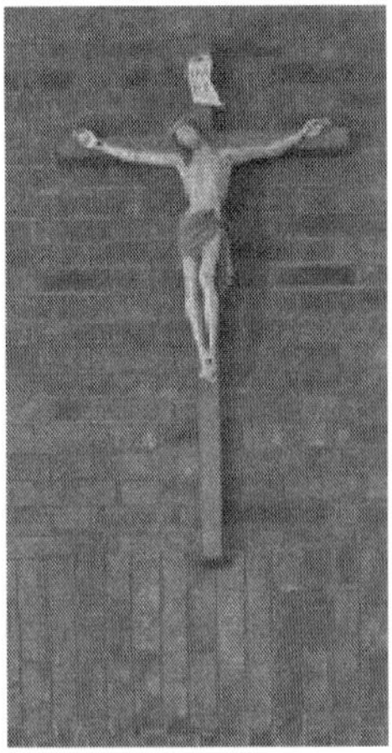

Centenary Crucifix

Epilogue

Over 100 years this community of Faith has grown and evolved from a handful of converts to a thriving Parish. This church 'family' has had its full share of life experiences meeting many and varied challenges. Their journey from open air Mass to temporary accommodation to permanent church is a testament of their perseverance and endurance. The current building is a memorial of National significance, primarily funded by public subscription and benefactors. It was the inspiration of a Priest who vowed to erect a 'Living Memorial' to the FEPOW of World War Two.

After the Second Vatican Council (1962-65) liturgical changes impacted on all aspects of the Church. Significantly, the role of the Laity was extended, particularly for women, and it also enabled and developed ecumenical dialogue between different faith groups.

Each generation has strived to live the Faith and ethos of Roman Catholicism against secular attitudes and pressures. It would be ironic if one of the future challenges for this Community of Faith was a parish without a resident priest; when a century ago Catholics had fervently prayed for one ...

There is no doubt that the next hundred years will be as much of a challenge to generations to come.

Date	Roll of **Priests**
c.1893 - 1904	Fr. Edmund Ford & Fr.G.Hughes of Beccles
1912 – Aug 1926	Priests from St.Johns, Norwich
1926 – Oct 1934	Fr.Thomas Kemp Phillips
1934 – Dec 1946	Fr.John Joseph Ketterer
Sep 1939	Assisted by: Walsingham Friars Minor
Sep 1941	Fr.Hulme
Feb 1942 -	Fr.Pitt
Nov 1942 -	Fr.O.Baker
1944 – Apr 1945	Fr. Bull
1946 – Aug 1965	Fr.Malcolm Leon Cowin
1965 - Oct 1975	Fr.Dennis Brophy
1975 - Feb 1983	Fr.Kenneth Stannard Chapman
1983 - Sep 1983	Fr. Joseph Farrell
1983 - Jun 1997	Fr.Peter Brown
1983 - 1988	Assisted by: (Q & A) Fr. Brendan Peters
1989 - 1992	Fr.Timothy Wright OSB
1985 - 1994	Sr. Dr.Alies Therese of Peace
1988 - 1992	(Q & A) Fr. Francis Selman
1992 - 1994	(Q & A) Fr.Timothy Brien
1994 - 1995	(Q & A) Fr.Carlos (from Venezuela)
1995 - 1995	(Q & A)Fr.Bernard Jones, O Carm
1995 - 2003	(Q) Fr.Roger Spencer
1997 - 2003	Fr.David Jennings
1998 - 2000	Assisted by: Fr.George Bennet MA
1999 - 2001	Fr. Con O'Brien (Rtd)
2002 - 2005	Deacon Peter Mahoney
	Sr.Teresa Talby SFCC
2003 – Jul 2005	Fr. Dr. Sean Connolly
2003 - 2005	Assisted by: Fr Gordon Cordy
	Deacon Peter Mahoney
Jul 2005–Sep 2005	Fr Brendan Moffat
2005 – to date	Fr. Richard White

(Q & A) Quidenham & Attleborough (Q) = Quidenham only

A Guild for Priests' Housekeepers
The Guild of Our Lady and St. Joseph
Constituted ca.1957
Set up to foster the vocational aspect of their work and to unite them by means of prayer and encourage mutual help and support. Wymondham's Housekeepers from this time belonged to this.

Wymondham Priests & Housekeepers

Date	Housekeeper	Priest	
1930	Mrs Kenny	Fr. Phillips	
c.1938-47	Adelaide Cross	Fr. Phillips	@ Sheringham
	Mrs Kenny	?Fr. Ketterer	
c.1945 –60? c.1960 - 65	?Miss Bailey ?Mrs Maud Cowin	Fr. Cowin	
c.1965 - ?	Miss Margaret Mooney Mrs Penny Rigby	Fr. Brophy	Came with Fr. Brophy Took over from her.
Ca.1980s	Miss Dorothy Scarfe Miss Dorothy Scarfe	Fr. Chapman Fr. Joe Farrell Fr. Peter Brown	Came with Fr. Chapman Miss Dorothy Scarfe. ? discontinued housekeeper services
			CWL did it on rota

Abbreviations

Bp. – Bishop
BSE – Bovine Spongiform Encephalitis
CaFÉ – Catholic Faith Exploration
Capt. – Captain
CWL – Catholic Women's League
FEPOW – Far East Prisoners of War
IRA – Irish Republican Army
KSC – Knights of St. Columba
MC – Military Cross; Also Master of Ceremonies (Head Altar Server)
PC – Parish Council (The Church's)
PP - Parish Priest
PPC – Parish Pastoral Council
RAMC – Royal Army Medical Corps
USAAF – United States Army Air Force
VE – Victory in Europe
VJ – Victory in Japan
VG – Vicar General
WWII – 2nd World War 1939-45
YTS – Youth Training Scheme

Bibliography

Bossy, J. (1996) *The English Catholic Community,* London, Darton, Longman & Todd

Hoare, Adrian (2004) *The Wymondham Story: A Snapshot History of a Market Town*, Norfolk, Wymondham Heritage Society

Johnstone, T. & Hagerty, J. (1996) *The Cross on the Sword* London, Geoffrey Chapman

Millard, Dom B (1989) 6th Edn. *The Book of Saints: A Dictionary of Servants of God Canonized by the Catholic Church,* London, A C Black Ltd.

Muir, M. (2006) *Emergency: Wymondham Emergency Training College for Teachers*, Norwich, Norfolk Archeological and Historical Research Group.

Reynolds, E.E. (1973) *The Roman Catholic Church in England and Wales: A Short History,* Hertfordshire, Anthony Clarke Books

Sansalone, J.Beck (2012) 2nd Edn. *'White Flak': Vignettes of a Franciscan Friar,* Cincinnati, OH, Regina Publishers

Standley, S. (2007) *In and around Wymondham then and now Vol.1*, Wymondham, Geo.R.Reeve.

Trappes-Lomax, T.B. (1950) *Diocese of Northampton Centenary Souvenir 1850 -1950,* London, Hoxton & Walsh (1918) Ltd.

Unknown, (1913) *A Great Gothic Fane,* London, Cranton & Ouseley, Ltd.

Yaxley, P.G. (1998) *Wymondham's Old Inns*, Norfolk, The Wymondham Society

Yaxley, P.G. (1999) *Wymondham: A Century Remembered* Norwich Nostalgia Publishing

Glossary of Terms

Aumbry – Holy Oils cabinet
Narthex –a large porch used as a Welcoming area in a modern church; originally at the western entrance and separated by a railing.
Tabernacle - the cabinet behind the altar in which the Blessed Sacrament is reserved
Reredos - decoration put up above and behind an altar.

Internet Addresses

www.fepow-memorial.org.uk
www.wymondham-rc-church.org.uk
Email – administrator@wymondham-rc-church.org.uk

All Enquiries to
The Parish Administrator ☏ 01953 601976
The RC Church of
Our Lady & St Thomas of Canterbury
1, Norwich Road
Wymondham
NR18 0QE